MW01290511

Copyright

For general information on the products and services
or for technical support, please contact directly to the
author :
Mobile : (+855)70 453 236
Email   : thavry@gmail.com

A Proper Woman

"A Proper woman" shows how important a communication is from generation to generation. And having a dream is the best way that we could go far as far as we want."

Thida Prak, Cambodia

"Each story clicks together very well, and it gives a sense of adventure. Anyway, I had a chance to taste a new form of ideas from "A Proper Woman" yet it's fresh and it's dramatically beautiful."

Dara Ly, Cambodia

"My journey with Thavry was deeply enhanced as I read her story. An inspiring insight bringing hope for a new generation of Cambodian, and young people everywhere. More than "A Proper Woman"–
a remarkable young woman."

Junette Burke, Australia

"Thavry's story is at times poignant, at times funny, but always enlightening and inspiring. She maps the path for many of this new Cambodian generation to follow and to see that while many traditions are important and should be preserved, others belong only in the past. Thavry has had an interesting life journey so far, and something tells me that she has many more adventures to come."

Iain Donnelly, Scotland

Thavry THON

"A Proper Woman gives a good picture of women's role in Cambodia. The author describes the society's tradition and history, at the same time as she describes her own place in it. Even if A Proper Woman is about growing up as a woman in Cambodia, you can as a woman, from anywhere in the world you may come from, recognize many of the scenarios in the book. In the end, this is a call for questioning of the patriarchate and an inspiration to crush it. If not for yourself, for your future daughter."

Malin Annie Jansson, Sweden

"A Proper Woman" is a refreshing story that encapsulates the resilience and determination of a woman as she challenges gender inequity. Thavry's journey plants a seed in readers, inspiring them to confront injustice and work diligently towards change. "

Layla Connolly, USA

"Raw, inspiring, moving. This extraordinary family portrait filled with drama, heartbreak and horror mirrors Cambodia's turbulent century. Demonstrating the power and resilience of women to bear the unbearable, to question the unquestionable, and to speak out against the unspeakable, Thavry's story sheds light on the struggles of women in Cambodia and the social norms and expectations that she is trying to break down."

Jessica Armstrong, Australia

A Proper Woman

"I understand how hard it is to follow our dreams. However, this is my first time that reading from the woman's point of view who was considered as a second priority. Her story is valuable for reading, both man and woman. Thank you for writing this book and I am so glad that Cambodia has a woman who dare to echo her voice for the other women."

Phraisohn Siripool, Thailand

"A powerful, fresh, catchy and unique autobiography that has a potential to inspire millions across the globe."

Tomas Hanak, Czech Republic

"I am so proud of the choices that she made along the way - her resilience, courage and defiance are an inspiration. I hope this book can help brothers, mothers, fathers and barangs understand the journey she and women like her took to understand the past and inspire hope for the future. For Thavry and women like her the best is yet to come."

Jam Ramjattan, Canada

"It is well written and the stories that tell about her grandmother, mother, and father and not least of her incredible journey are so interesting and deeply moving. They are very particular but at the same time tell a lot about Cambodian history, culture and traditions."

Magnus Saemundsson, Sweden

Thavry THON

"**A Proper Woman**" is a beautiful story linking Cambodia's tragic past with its complex yet hopeful future. Authors like **Thavry Thon** will serve as an inspiration not just to young women in Cambodia, but around the world.

Adam Vaught, USA

A Proper Woman

"A Proper Woman" written by **Miss Thavry Thon** is a sibling book of "**DARA LY** Reading Standard" written by **Mr. Dara Ly**.

If you have "**DARA LY** Reading Standard" in your right hand, then perhaps you should have "**A Proper Woman**" in your left hand.

A Proper Woman

"Life is a beautiful and wonderful gift"

THAVRY THON

A Proper Woman

Contents

Dedication

This book is dedicated with love and respect to my family who have had such a huge impact on my life. I want to thank my mother, who has shared with me the stories of her life that have helped to give me a better perspective on the challenges that women in Cambodia have overcome, and what still needs to be done. Thank you to my father, who has always been such a brave and courageous man, and has supported me in whatever I have done. And last but not least, I thank you my two encouraging brothers.

I could not have lived the life I have, nor written this book about it, without the loving support from each of you.

Thavry THON

Acknowledgements

I have received incredible support from many people during the writing of this book. I wish to give special mention to two whose kindness and help have made this book as clear, strong and engaging as it is, with whom I wrote much of the initial drafts.

Peter Ford, my editor. Thank you for your kind heart and willingness to help me with editing all of my notes into this fantastic book. You have had such a huge impact on the book, and without your dedication it would certainly not be the same. I greatly enjoyed reading over and over the edits you made and answering your detailed questions. I am proud to call you my friend.

Charles Di Bella, my mentor. Your guidance and encouragement in helping me believe in myself and pursue my dreams has been central to my life since we first met. Your love and concern for me and my family has given all of us support and strength in difficult times. Thank you.

SmallWorld Cambodia. This oasis of calm in northern

Phnom Penh has always inspired me, and is where I have met so many wonderful like-minded people. Working at this start-up hub has given me a place where I can be myself, and it where so much of this book was written. It is somewhere I can honestly call my second home.

Preface

Being born and raised in rural Cambodia has ensured I have had quite an interesting life.
80% of Cambodia's population live in rural areas, and that's where I was born and raised.

Although my parents have let me have the freedom to do what I love, Cambodia's deeply ingrained social norms have still have had a strong impaction on me and my family members.

For as long as I can remember, I have asked myself why women obey so many ingrained rules concerning the role and proper conduct of women. Why must women be kept dependant on men for their livelihoods, married young by their parents without any choice and kept from pursuing education that might let them live a different life?

When I return to the village I grew up in, many of the young girls I used to be an English tutor for are now married with children. They have followed the path that their mothers most likely followed before them, the traditional expectations for women in many countries; to marry young, to have children, to support your husband.

The girls I know have been unable to explore the wider world around them, or pursue their dreams or passions, as we all should be able to. I have been able to travel to many countries in Europe, America and Asia. I managed to make these journeys by believing in my dreams and working hard to achieve them.

With the support of my parents, I was able to challenge the traditional norms in my village, and have been able to show that women are capable of doing many great things when given the chance. Daring to question the social realities was not always easy, but I am very glad that I have, and will continue to do so. Still, there were many difficulties because I am living in a strict society that still follows outdated cultural norms. Every actions I took, I felt like there were always some watching eyes and criticisms. Yet I still did what my heart desired. Cambodia is a country in transition, with rapid economic development and growing international ties coexisting with our resilient culture and history.

In 2016 economic growth remained stable at 6.9% thanks to strong performances by the garment, construction, and tourism sectors. This change is threatening many long-held beliefs and practices, and gender equality is slowly improving, but has a long way to go. It has been a long journey for me to gather up enough courage to write this book.

I wrote this book in the hope of inspiring and encouraging young women to hold on to their dreams, to believe in themselves and be confident that they are capable of doing so much more than society often expects of them.

We each are capable of doing amazing things when we receive the same support as our brothers, and this book is proof of that.

Introduction

Cambodian society has always been rigid. The country's rich culture, traditions and adherence to Buddhism has remained largely intact since the pinnacle of the Angkorian civilization for which Cambodia is famous. For older generations, including that of my parents, adherence to the strict rules that all people had to follow was unquestioned.

In a country where 32 percent of the population is under 14 years of age, a growing number of people were not directly affected by the turmoil and civil war that dominated Cambodia for much of the last 40 years. This social evolution and drive for change, aided by largely unhindered access to the internet and improvements in education means that a new generation of Cambodians is seeking equality and agency that was simply not possible before. This is especially apparent when it comes to gender equality and women's rights.

My grandmother never attended school, and had to perform household chores at home with her mother and sisters while her brothers had the privilege of attending school. Her mother did not allow her to study, believing that education was not for girls.

Such social rules have been applied worldwide for centuries. Whatever the stated reason, they have had the effect of controlling women and stifling our hopes, dreams and abilities. My grandmother was married at 16, with little more expected of her than looking after the house and children. Because she was uneducated herself she did not understand the value of education in others, and so she treated my mother the same as her own mother had treated her. She discouraged my mother from acquiring an education.

But my mother was strong. She loved attending the school her father insisted she attend.
Her father wanted her to have a better future, and be independent. Her dream of becoming a primary school teacher was quashed by her mother's demands to earn money by weaving mattresses and by working at the farm, and to pay for her brothers' education. Her marriage at 21 was arranged, and that put an end to any chance of living her life as freely as she had wanted to. Instead, she began living her dreams through her children, ensuring that they had the freedom to walk a different path to her own, and the opportunities to be whoever they wanted to be.

My mother would always remind me that education is the most precious treasure anyone can have. She supported me in my pursuit of higher education, and encouraged me every step of the way. I was not forced into an arranged marriage, and after generations of such subservience to social practices that seem to only benefit men, I am the first woman in my family to break this cycle.

I understand that true gender equality in Cambodia is still a long way off, but it is also an inalienable human right that women be valued equal to men. As a woman born and raised in an unequal society, I feel the pain of the millions denied this right, and I want to speak out for the countless women who feel they have no voice. I want to inspire and encourage them to believe in their dreams and be who they want to be, regardless of the expectations of other people.

I had to break many of the centuries-old traditions in my village to attain my own freedom to follow my dreams, but I knew I had to. Women are able to accomplish great things when given the opportunity, and it is a beautiful feeling to do what you love, rather than what is expected of you by society.

I do not believe Cambodians should simply adopt foreign cultural practices in place of our own, but I do feel that our gender roles are unjust. Our society must begin to evolve, to treat women with the fairness, respect and equality all human beings deserve, while still being true to our culture. But there is a long way

yet to go.
I hope readers will find my story both interesting and enlightening.

If you are a woman I hope you will find inspiration and encouragement to do what you love and be who you are. You are not alone as you experience the unfairness and inequality all around you.

If you are man, I hope you will gain a better understanding of how it feels to live under such unfair and rigid social realities. Not only just to understand the issues, but to take action, to pay better respect to women, your wife, your mother, and your sisters, and to speak up in support of equal rights.

Chapter 1: A Shattered Childhood

*"It takes time to heal these wounds,
but life must move on"*

*This is the last time that my mother saw her father when he
came to visit the family*

In the years before the Khmer Rouge came to power in Cambodia, my mother, then a young girl, led a relatively charmed life and was lovingly spoiled by my grandfather. He took her with him most days as he went about his working day, eating fancy breakfasts together. Her father always ordered the Chinese noodle soup with pork for her, and the coffee and sweet milk with bread. During those times, only the rich could normally afford to eat such a breakfast.

He bought her a nice dress, skirt and shirt, and a golden bracelet and necklace. She was like a little princess, born on the island of Koh Ksach Tunlea, on the Bassac River in southern Cambodia. This did not mean that she didn't study hard at school. Indeed, she loved going to school and this was reflected in regularly finishing top of her class among 40 students. Her father ensured she attended every day, he helped her with her homework and exam revision, with a big reward each month like buying new jewellery or new clothes.

Her life changed, however, when he was killed by Khmer Rouge soldiers in March 1975, a month before the end of the civil war between the government and the communist forces of Pol Pot's Khmer Rouge. His work as a judge at Kandal provincial court, and therefore his association with the government, had made him a target for the Khmer Rouge. Not that he supported the government. In fact, with a group of friends and colleagues he had set up a small local political party in 1974 intended to better the lives of Cambodians and seek peace.

She was about 10 years old, and her brother just 27 days old when their father was killed.

One day, her father came to visit the family and he was walking down to the river with my mother on his shoulders. After he came back, two men came to the house and asked him to go with them. He left without saying a word and was never seen again. My mother was shocked and crying watching her father walk away from his home. She screamed to him – "Father! When will you come back?" Everyone in the house was very scared that the Khmer Rouge soldiers knew their family background. My mother had to learn how to live by herself, to keep safe and out of trouble.

Anyone associated with the former government of General Lon Nol was liable for arbitrary execution. This included my grandfather. The Khmer Rouge labeled civil servants, teachers and members of the armed forces as enemies of the new regime, which instead envisioned an agrarian utopia in which all were equal and classless.

Money was banned, and cities were emptied as people were forcibly marched into the countryside. Respect for "Angkar," the name used to describe the Khmer Rouge bureaucracy, was paramount and people were encouraged to spy on their neighbors to ensure conformity. People stopped trusting each other. People hid their background; they did not want to share the truth with other people because they were scared of being killed. Children were taught that Angkar represented their true parents.

My mother was put to work far away from what remained of her family, and organised schooling was stopped. Instead, classes became an informal affair, with older children sharing what they knew in moments of rest. She had to wake up at 4 am, and would be woken with a bucket of water dumped on her if she overslept. She would then go to work in the rice fields until noon. Her task was to build up the walls of the paddies to ensure they stored enough water. Each morning, she had to build 1.5 meters of the walls, and the same height each afternoon.

The work was very difficult, and the food so meagre that she was soon very thin. At the communal dining hall each morning she was given one corn cob before beginning almost 12 hours of work. For lunch, a thin soup was given, which only contained about one spoonful of rice. It was like food scraps given to animals, but she had to accept the fact that life had changed. She needed to fight to survive.

She was not completely alone however, as her two younger brothers Hak, aged five, and Chen, seven, were also in the children's work group with her. Their role was to collect the dung from cows and water buffalo all day, which was used as fertilizer for the rice fields. Her 17-year-old sister Chansok however had been sent to a work camp for teenagers in Tuol Krosang village, some 17 kilometers away. Her youngest brother was just a baby and was kept with her grandmother.

She was only allowed to visit her family once a week, and had to leave early in the morning in order to return to the children's camp in time for work the following day. They were kept about 7 kilometers west of the island, and she would cross the river on a small boat, rowed by a Khmer Rouge soldier, walking the rest of the way for the brief visit, before retracing the journey at night back to the camp.

The never ending work, the inadequate food, the distance from her mother and the complete change in the life she was used to meant that she became more and more miserable. As the daughter of an educated man – especially one associated with the previous government killed on the orders of Angkar – she and her family were constantly spied upon and monitored, not just by Khmer Rouge soldiers, but by their neighbours.

Cambodia has a rich mixture of different ethnic groups including the dominant Khmer, the Chinese, the Muslim Cham, and various smaller groups in the mountains. However, its Vietnamese community has long been marginalized, and this was especially true under the Khmer Rouge. My mother was of mixed Vietnamese and Chinese heritage, and this meant that in addition to all of the suspicion around her father's former profession, she and her family were treated as a lower class of citizen.

Despite living not far from the same rural community she was born and had grown up in – rural Cambodians were called 'base' under the Khmer Rouge – she was treated as one of the 'new people,' the term used to describe the deportees from Cambodia's cities who were treated especially harshly due to their exposure to corrupting modern ideas. In an effort to protect her family as much as possible, my grandmother worked as hard as she could, to appear valuable to the Khmer Rouge.

Several of my mother's family on her father's side were killed between 1975 and 1979. Three of her cousins died while serving as child soldiers for the Khmer Rouge, and my mother found the identity and photograph of one of them in the record at the infamous S-21 Genocide Museum in Phnom Penh, where soldiers deemed traitorous were tortured and killed nearby.

Her uncle, another soldier, died of starvation in Pursat province.

Several were killed on her mother's side as well. An uncle, my grandmother's oldest brother, was killed along with his wife and three children because of her Chinese descent and inability to speak the Khmer language very well. They were all taken to Koh Kor, an island in the Saang district set aside as a prison, where they all died from either torture or execution. My grandmother's brother-in-law and his son died from starvation when they were relocated to Pursat province.

At least fourteen of my mother's relatives died during the regime. The number would certainly have been higher, but my grandmother destroyed all of the family photos and documents by throwing them in the Bassac River, which hindered soldiers efforts to identify additional family members. Dissociating themselves from my grandfather meant they survived.

The Khmer Rouge had a saying: "In order to cut the grass, you have to remove the roots." This meant that if one of your family was identified as having worked for the Lon Nol government, other family members would also be arrested, and likely killed. In my mother's case, while she was spared execution, she had to work twice as hard to please the soldiers, to prove that she was useful for Angkar.

Three years, eight months and twenty days under the Khmer Rouge was a nightmare that seemed to my mother to last an eternity. She lived in fear. She often wondered if she would survive until the next day; what if she did something wrong in Angkar's eyes? What would happen to her siblings and family?

Lost in the daily drudgery of rice farming she thought back fondly to the life she had lead before. What if there had been no war, would she still be her father's little princess, wearing nice clothes and eating delicious foods?

Her entire world had been turned upside down – as had the whole country. The Khmer Rouge had intentionally tried to return the country to a mythical time, when all were equal and lives were spent farming in rural communities. Fridges and cars, examples of the western decadence that had corrupted Cambodia, were stacked into piles in the cities and abandoned, as were the cities themselves.

Cambodian families are traditionally large and tight-knit. Cousins and relatives live close by, and religious festivals offer the chance to gather. The Khmer Rouge put an end to that. The banning of Buddhism, the forced cross-country migrations and the high number of deaths that occurred either directly or by the harsh conditions they enforced, all combined to shatter century-old ways of life. Women became single mothers, children became orphans. Homes were destroyed, communities uprooted and strangers made of neighbours.

In the early 1970's, villages in Cambodia were largely unchanged from how they might have looked a hundred years before. Simple wooden houses, ox-carts and unpaved roads, all surrounded by rice fields. Schooling, if it occurred, was mostly done by monks at the pagoda, and government interference in daily life was minimal.

Under the Khmer Rouge, however, all this changed. What had once been private property, including food supplies, was now strictly controlled by Angkar. Nothing was private and human life became seemingly of little value. Cruelty abounded. Even after hearing the stories of my relatives and neighbours, I still cannot imagine life during this period. But I am amazed with my mother's bravery, and that she survived the conditions under which she was forced to live and work.

On January 7, 1979, Vietnamese forces – aided by former Khmer Rouge soldiers who had fled internal purges, including Prime Minister Hun Sen – succeeded in pushing out the Khmer Rouge and liberating Cambodia from its hardship.

People slowly began to be reunited with what was left of their families. While the horror was over, the scars in people's minds and hearts remained, and does so to this day. The country had experienced a shared nightmare, and for the newly freed Cambodians like my mother, they felt it was like a rebirth. A new life had begun and my mother's life was safer, but certainly not any easier.

With most of the country's educated citizens either dead or in exile abroad, and the infrastructure devastated, in many ways the country had to begin again from scratch.

One of the first public services to restart was the country's schools. With the Khmer Rouge having destroyed the central role that Buddhist monks had played in educating those rural Cambodians lucky enough to receive some sort of education, the country now began to adopt a Vietnamese style of state-run education.

My mother was able to restart her studies and she still loves to tell me how good a student she was, top of all of her classes, despite no support from her own mother.

In 1980 she began classes at Por Thivong Primary School, not far from her house, but without her father's support she had to fight her mother to attend, as she struggled to see the value in educating my mother, as she herself had not attended school. My grandmother insisted my mother work to support the family rather than waste her time studying.

A trade-off was agreed upon, with my mother attending class in the mornings – sitting at the front of the class in her tattered clothes – and the rest of the day spent in the rice field, or fishing to feed the family. I often imagined her in class, very skinny, half of her brain excited about class, the other half nervous about if she would be allowed to be in class the next day.

Through her stories, and her pushing myself and my two brothers to try hard at school, I grew up knowing how important education could be. This was such a contrast to how my grandmother treated learning.

My grandmother had never learnt to read or write, neither had my great grandmother, and I assume all of my family's women before them as well.

My grandmother viewed education as a male pursuit, the prevailing belief in Cambodia at the time. Her brothers had gone to school, while she and her sister stayed at home. She once explained to me the excuse her mother had given her for this arrangement.

"My mother did not allow me to go to school because she was afraid I would write love letters to a secret boyfriend. I had to be at home and help raise the pigs, and go to farm rice. Instead of learning I had to work hard."

While she may have truly believed the love letter excuse, her persistence to prevent my mother from pursuing an education was just a sad reminder of the role of women in Cambodia in those days, which had remained largely unchanged for centuries.

My mother had been able to break the cycle of illiteracy that women in my family had experienced before her. My mother's generation was the first to gain tentative access to education, and a greater role in society, and mine has capitalised upon this. There is still a long way to go before there is true equality in Cambodia, as in much of the world, but the way older women talk of the past, sounds like another planet.

Life was so difficult for them, not being able to read or write. Shop signs, food packaging, newspapers, all were unintelligible. They missed out on the social interaction of classmates and friends at school, the group activities and games, and the important life lessons school provides.

Generations of females were raised to be secondary to men. They were left at home, denied even local travel, and this all contributed in maintaining Cambodia's conservative social practices.

Arranged marriage was one such manifestation of this. While not unique to Cambodia, the practice has proven resilient in the face of French colonial rule, civil war, the Khmer Rouge and Vietnamese occupation.

My grandmother once asked my mother why she was so interested in studying, as she would soon be someone's wife. By implication, this meant she would become a farmer and housewife, and that none of what she was learning would be important. But she was determined to study, despite the lack of encouragement.

She finished her primary schooling in 1982, and passed the exams to allow her to progress to secondary school, which at the time only went up to grade 7. Her dream at the time was to become a primary school teacher, which would require her to finish up to grade 7, then take a one-year course at teacher training school.

The need to move schools however, meant there were now more challenges standing in her way. As she lived on an island, attending secondary school would involve crossing onto the mainland. In addition to needing access to a boat she also needed to provide her own school desk and uniform, which was expensive for a poor rural family supported by a single parent.

The war had stripped the family of any of their former wealth, and my grandmother's resistance to my mother's study duly increased, as she was far more occupied with her daily challenge to grow enough food to feed four children and her own elderly mother. Education was not a priority for her daughters, yet she let all of her sons continue their learning.

Yet my mother did not give up. She had really made an impression with her primary school teacher, Mr. Thorn, and he visited the house to try to negotiate for her to be allowed to continue her studies.

My grandmother was reluctant, but Mr. Thorn was persistent, and he eventually convinced her of the value of allowing my mother to continue to study. He bought her the required uniform, books and desk. The 4,000 riel (about $25 today) school fee was a cost my mother had to meet though, which she did by weaving sleeping mats in the little spare time she had after helping her mother in the rice field.

Her new school, which drew students from all of the villages in the area, had four classrooms which each sat about 40 students. Over 70 percent were boys, and my mother joined two other girls from her island.

She would get up at 5am, and eat some leftover rice for breakfast, before joining her friends waiting for the sail boat. After four hours of lessons each morning, she would walk about 4km to her family's rice field, and spend up to 10 hours working there. She came home every day exhausted, and she remained very skinny, and had regular arguments with her mother over the amount of farm work she was able to do, sometimes resulting in beatings with a wooden stick. Yet she was adamant that she would not quit to please her mother, and remained happy that she was able to continue her studies.

That does not mean she wasn't jealous of the life she once had, or of other members of her family who had come through the Khmer Rouge period with less death and turmoil. Her father's brother had survived. So had her four female cousins, who lived about 1km away and experienced a more comfortable existence, wearing nice clothes and having better food to eat. Their attendance at school had not been fought for, or even questioned.

After completing grades 5 and 6, my mother was unfortunately stopped from taking her final exams, just two months before the end of grade 7. Her farming commitments had meant that she hadn't had the time and energy to study as much as she once had, and falling grades had been enough to convince my grandmother that her attendance at school was a folly.

So instead of graduating and becoming a primary school teacher, or a civil servant or doctor like many of her classmates, she had to follow in her mother's footsteps and farm rice. While they went on to become comfortably wealthy, using their education to find well paying and influential jobs, my mother did not.

"I did not have any relatives or even my own mother to inspire me to study, guide me, or tell me that studying hard would be good for me in the future, but I had tried as hard as I could to have that education," she told me once.

"I still regret that I was not able to wait until the exam and then apply to be a teacher as I dreamed. If my father were there, I would have been able to study all the way and not cared about working at the field. I regret about the end of my education. I was one of the smartest kids in school, but the result now is that I am just a farmer."

As a daughter she was neither expected, nor encouraged, to attend school. In contrast the attendance of her two brothers, who also had no farming tasks, was not questioned.

I cannot imagine the challenges and disappointments my mother has had to live through in her life. Her once comfortable early childhood disrupted by the Khmer Rouge, and her dreams of becoming a teacher quashed by her own mother.

As the first woman in her family to stand up for her right to an education, what she was not able to achieve in her own childhood, she strove to realise in mine. I am very grateful for how she treated her own daughter's education.

She fought against the prevailing social norms and very nearly won. I am very lucky indeed.

My mother worked as a child labour

Chapter 2: Social Norms For Women

"Women are not designed to just get married and make babies"

Since I was a young girl, I have asked myself the question "what does it mean to be a proper woman?"

Cambodia has strong tradition of enforcing cultural norms pertaining to women – how they should look, act, think – and even as a child I questioned these, pushed back, dared to discover what would happen if I broke the rules.

My mother used to tell me stories about how girls in Cambodia used to have to perform all of the household chores such as cooking, cleaning and weaving and only rarely left the house. Women were not permitted to talk openly with men, and any form of education was a rare luxury.

Based on her own experiences growing up, where she too had to do lots of chores while her brother didn't, when it came to raising her own children my brothers and I were all expected to help around the house.

Even with the rich cultural diversity in Cambodia – Khmer, Viet, Thai, Lao, Chinese, Cham,and local minority groups – a set of strict rules governing female behaviors have long been widely followed and rarely questioned.

My great grandmother was Vietnamese, and as she was never educated, her ability to speak Khmer was severely limited. She spoke Vietnamese at home. In this socially and linguistically sheltered world she was not raised to question the role of women. As such, my grandmother was not sent to school, largely because my great grandmother had not been.

Being uneducated creates a very difficult life. When one's only way to look at the world is based on what you can see in front of you, it is hard to imagine different ways of doing things, different experiences, a different life. She could not even feel jealousy for her brothers attending school, as she knew that girls didn't go to school. Instead, she and her younger sister spent all day doing housework and farming tasks.

Cambodian society placed the value of education squarely on men, in addition to their perceived physical strengths. In contrast, female weakness was compounded by the dependency of being uneducated. Women would be married at a young age, as it was believed that a man needed to look after them, that they couldn't survive as an adult without a husband. Even for my mother's generation it was common to be married before 20 – and for some minority groups it still is – and I think that the lack of critical thinking taught in school meant that few questioned this arrangement.

When I heard stories of these young arranged marriages I would often wonder if there was any love involved, or were they purely for security. Women got married in order to have a man to look after and provide for them, while men married to produce children. Talking with my grandmother and mother I struggled to find a deeper reasoning than that.

My grandmother got married when she was 16 to a man who was 30, but their marriage was not the typical arranged style common at the time. My grandfather, a tall, handsome, educated judge had been in contact with my grandmother before the wedding. This was scandalous and caused many people in the village to gossip and pass judgement. The union was also not supported by his own family, who were far wealthier and better educated than my grandmother. None of this affected their desire to wed, and so they ignored the criticisms and started building their family.

When my grandmother was 17, after a year of marriage, they had their first baby, but the baby did not survive the ordeal. It was hard for my grandmother to lose her first baby. Time passed, she moved on. She stayed at home, cooking and cleaning and following the dreary routine of a housewife.

It was not until 6 years later that they had their next child. Aunt Chansok thankfully survived, and through her my grandmother was able to transfer all of the lessons about life that she had learnt from her mother. Three years later my mother was born, a tiny white-skinned girl with mixed Vietnamese and Chinese blood.

The positions of class and family status in Cambodia at the time were very strict. My grandfather's mother never accepted my grandmother due to her low status, and in fact never let her address her as "mother." She wanted my grandfather to marry someone at least equally as wealthy, although her husband had no such concerns. My great grandmother refused to accept these females into her family.

I never met my great grandmother of my grandfather's side. She died from food poisoning and diarrhoea. There were no photographs survived the Khmer Rouge years. I have often wondered what she looked like, did she have a stern face? Is that why she was so strict with my grandmother? From what I have been told she had the small eyes and pale skin of the Cambodian-Chinese, and was a shrewd business lady – saving her takings from selling sapodilla fruit to become one of the richest ladies in the village.

She was able to hire many people to pick the fruit, and transport it for her via boat to Vietnam. The income meant her family lived a comfortable life, and all of four of her sons received full educations. Yet despite the attention she paid to her own children, time did not change her feelings towards my grandparents and mother. They directly suffered from the strict social norms that my great grandmother was intent on enforcing.

My mother remembers having to wash sapodilla fruit when she visited her grandmother's house, not being able to play as her cousins could. She attributes this to my great grandmother's view that the women in her son's family were beneath her, were only fit as staff, not family. My mother grew up receiving little love from her father's side.

This did not deter my grandmother, who still tried to be civil and be accepted into the family, and it slowly led to a partial softening of her stance, but never the full inclusion she wanted.

Her daily life was spent like most women in Cambodia, at home taking care of the children and minding the family farm. My grandfather's salary at the court had been about $1,500 in today's terms, a very large amount, especially for a rural setting. It allowed him to support his family very well. His death meant that the life they were able to lead after 1979 was very different to what they had known before.

My mother's requirement to put her family first, before her education, was especially hard for her. Gone was the nice food, instead the poor family had to mix corn with their rice just to get enough to eat. My mother and her brothers would go fishing when they could find the time to supplement the meagre fare.

Travel for women was traditionally difficult in Cambodia, and this did not improve much by the 1980s. My mother never travelled further than to secondary school when she was a child, and women across the country were warned not to travel far, as it was too dangerous for them. Whether or not this was actually true – Cambodia in the 1980s was still a very dangerous place with Khmer Rouge guerrillas fighting the army – the fear was ever present and often repeated, and stopped women from exploring their surroundings, much as the limits on education limited their academic explorations.

Even as a teenager, when she had more responsibility to support the family, she did not travel far. She now had a bicycle, and would ride this to neighboring villages – escorted by her brother-in-law – to exchange her woven mattresses for rice. In the early 1980s the use of money had still not fully recovered its banning by the Khmer Rouge, and in rural areas bartering was widespread.

Despite her battles to receive an education, and to escape from the confines of traditional village life, my mother had failed. She had tried to challenge the social expectations for women, and had done this without any close role models. Instead of becoming the teacher she wanted to be she was stuck in the village, farming rice and weaving mats. To add insult to injury, the money she earned went towards her brothers' continued education.

Yet my mother was strong and had not given up fighting for what she instinctively felt was a better, fairer position for women. While she had been unable to pursue her dream career she ensured that her children had no such restrictions, and for that I am eternally grateful.

I wish my mother could have finished her schooling. I wish she had had more freedom within her own family, and society at large, but life for her generation was far stricter than mine.

I do not know how I would have reacted if I had been presented with the same hurdles and barriers that she faced. Would I have fought like she did? Would I have fought harder, or accepted 'realities' sooner? It is impossible to tell, as I thankfully have never had to face all that she did as a child. I am immensely proud of everything she achieved.

Chapter 3: A Child Soldier For The Khmer Rouge

"His hand deserved to hold a pen, not a gun"

My father was forced to be the child solider for Khmer Rouge

While some of the social expectations and 'rules' have been perpetuated and repeated by women – such as my great grandmother – I thought it was important to highlight some of the men who have, through their actions, fought the system, and encouraged their sisters, wives and daughters to do the same.

My father is one such man and he has had a large impact on who I am today. Together with my mother, they have supported me and my two brothers in our education, and in all that we have wished to do.
So in the spirit of fairness and equality that he has instilled in me. His own childhood and the challenges he faced and overcame in his life.

In the early 1990s, more than a decade after the Khmer Rouge had been largely driven from Cambodia, there was still fighting in the country. Re-armed and re-trained (with American, UK, Chinese and ASEAN support), Khmer Rouge soldiers had returned over the border from bases in Thailand to attack government forces and terrorize the Cambodian population.

This was the context with which I spent my early years, although all I remember from this is not having much food to eat, rather than any danger, and our family was happy and safe on the island.

After dinner most evenings, my father would sit in his hammock under our stilted house, while my older brother Rithy and I would sit on the ground and listen to his stories. He always told us the same fairy tale over and over again, but we never grew bored of listening and always had questions to ask.

Growing up with two brothers, I had a rather adventurous childhood, climbing trees or fishing – activities decidedly 'unfeminine' but enormous fun, and something my parents allowed me to do without criticism or hinderance.

My dad would always put me up on his shoulder as he walked to the farm, and from my high perch I would ask him to explain what we walked past, the names of plants, trees and lakes. I remembered he showed the guava leaves are for curing diarrhoea, and neem tree leaves and bark reduced fever, but it is very bitter. He was a fountain of knowledge, explaining which plants were medicinal or edible, a knowledge he gained as a child soldier for the Khmer Rouge, a period of his life that did not only shape his own life, but also very much who I am today.

I grew up by listening to his repeated stories about the Khmer Rouge until I came to remember them all. When I was younger and didn't want to finish the food on my plate, he would remind me that during his own childhood he had had to do many things he didn't want to, just to survive, so the least I could do was finish the food, and be grateful for the simple things – a message that remains with me to this day.

My father's family name is Thul. He has dark skin, big eyes, curly hair and is tall compared to most Cambodian men. He grew up in a very large family, the second oldest of his nine siblings, on the same island as my mother, but on the opposite side. After his elder brother died, at some point after 1975 after being conscripted into the Khmer Rouge army, my father became the oldest son, and with it gained certain responsibilities.

In 1976, during the early years of Khmer Rouge control, my father was nine. Despite the mass relocations of people across the country, his family had been allowed to stay on the island. But in 1977, he was moved 15 km away, and made to carry dirt to build the Prek Rang dam. This was intended to help store excess rainy season water and thus allow for a second yearly rice harvest, part of Khmer Rouge policy to boost rice production and with it national self sufficiency.

This task he performed every day for two years, until early-1978, when armed clashes with Vietnamese soldiers along the southern and eastern borders began to increase. While Vietnam had once been allies of the Khmer Rouge, and had had an important role in their creation and initial training, the geopolitical ramifications of the Sino-Soviet split – the Khmer Rouge were closely supported by China, while Vietnam looked to the Soviet Union – and lingering centuries-old tensions had led to frequent border clashes by 1978.

In a desperate attempt to defend against the far larger and better equipped Vietnamese forces, my father was made into a child backline soldier. Due to his age and size, he was too small to carry a gun, and instead was made to transport supplies of rice and ammunition to the frontline troops throughout the dry season.

As the rains of July arrived he was transfered to grow rice to feed the troops. Far from his family, his overriding desire to survive allowed him to endure the long and difficult working days.

In the first few days of January 1979, he was moved to Phnom Den, a village in Takeo province very close to the Vietnamese border. This time, age 12, he was given a gun and told to fight the Vietnamese troops massing on the other side of the border but the Khmer Rouge soldiers proved no match for the Vietnamese, battle hardened after their decades-long wars against French, American and Chinese invasion. After only a few days his unit had retreated and Phnom Penh was captured by Vietnamese troops and the Khmer Rouge defectors on January 7.

It took about three months for the Vietnamese to say they had gained control of the country, with only pockets of Khmer Rouge left in the forests near the Thai border. Most had fled to Thailand, or thrown off their uniforms and gone back home.

After six months of slowly walking across the western part of Cambodia, including three months spent in the Cardamom mountains, my father's unit ended up in the border town of Pailin, famous for the gems mined in the province and a lasting holdout for the Khmer Rouge until the late 90s. Having actively engaged the Vietnamese soldiers in combat – but not killing any he always stresses – my father was equally as scared of the invaders as of the Khmer Rouge. His impulse was simply to return to his home and family, but if he did that his own unit would kill him, and so he stayed and followed orders.

The invasion had compounded the already challenging task of feeding the country. The exhausted population was barely able to produce enough food just to sustain life, and early 1979 was one of extreme hunger for much of the famine hit country. For Khmer Rouge soldiers holed up in the mountains, it was impossible to receive supplies of rice and they had to scavenge for plants, roots and leaves. My father became thinner, with the days feeling longer and nighttime especially seemingly to last forever. He describes this period as hell, as he was slowly and painfully starving to death.

It came to a point where he felt that running away posed a greater chance of survival than staying with his unit, so together with a few friends they left the forests of Pailin province in late 1979 to find food. Walking east, towards the center of Cambodia, they crossed mountains and forests before arriving in Pursat province, and were promptly captured by Vietnamese soldiers.

Rumours circulated amongst the Khmer Rouge had painted Vietnamese soldiers as very cruel, and my father fully believed they would cut his throat at the earliest moment. He soon realised this had just been propaganda designed to reduce desertion, as not only did they not kill him but he was taken to an orphanage where he was fed and clothed.

The staff at the orphanage asked him about his family, but by this stage, my father had no idea where they were or even if they were still alive. Due to the insular nature of island life, and limited access to the greater community, he was also unsure of where exactly he had grown up and so he stayed on in Pursat town.

For a year he lived with a foster family, who slowly managed to restore hope and joy for life in him and his reintegration back into normal society. They treated him as their own child, and as such he performed the chores expected of one, feeding their water buffalo and helping on the farm. Indeed, they had taken him in so that he might perform the tasks of their missing teenaged son.

While he enjoyed his new life away from the fighting, he still missed his family and harboured dreams of returning to them. Despite offers to stay permanently as the newest member of the foster family, as the year progressed he increasingly wanted to try to find his own.

With little more than vague recollections of his former home, somewhere to the south of Phnom Penh, he set out on a bicycle the family had bought him. While today the journey takes half a day by car, the more than 200 km was decidedly more difficult in 1981, with the roads still damaged by war, and it took him three days.

His foster mother's brother had cycled with him, and not knowing really where they were going, they just followed the rivers south – first the Tonle Sap, then the Tonle Bassac – in the hope that he would recognise his island home. Not that their combined observation skills were up to much, as after two days they somehow managed to cycle through Phnom Penh, home to more than a million people, without realising they were in the capital.

Continuing south they reached Takamo town, the provincial capital and somewhere that he says he sensed he was close to home, and arrived a day later.

Following the Tonle Bassac on National Road 21, the pair soon reached the market in Saang district, a place my father remembered visiting a few times as a young child, and from here he knew it wasn't far to Koh Ksach Tunlea island.

In 1981, at the age of 14, and five years after he had been forced to leave his home, my father had returned. Despite locals insisting that everyone had either died or moved away from the island, he persevered, and finally found his way to Kbal Koh Lech village, and was amazed to discover his father and family still alive.

They did not recognize the tall, skinny youth at first having assumed he was dead. But he was finally home, and his family proceeded to make the biggest party they could to celebrate his return. It meant parting ways with his foster family, but they kept in touch, and he last saw his foster mother in 1999 when she came to visit him the island, and I was very honored to meet her.

War is incredibly cruel to both soldiers and civilians. Those waging it care only for killing and defeating their enemy, those fleeing care only for survival. Civil war is possibly even crueler, splitting families and communities, and even then by forcing former enemies to live together. It creates parents without children, and children without parents.

My father was considered one of the lucky children. Despite having been forced into combat and almost starving to death, he had not been injured. He had fled the Vietnamese and hidden in forests hundreds of kilometers from home. He had escaped the Khmer Rouge and been captured. Yet he had survived, and returned to his hometown and his family.

His elder brother had also been made a child soldier, but he did not return home after the war. After years of waiting for him to also one day appear in the village, the family are resigned to the fact that he has died.

The war years taught my father many things, not just about survival but also about human nature – and human cruelty – but his strongest lesson is that he never wishes to experience war again or to be separated from his family.

Chapter 4: My Mother's Arranged Marriage

"Marriage is a lifetime commitment, so make it right"

My grandfather on my father's side came to ask my grand-mother

As was common for most women in Cambodia until very recently, my mother was forced to accept an arranged marriage.But who or what was to blame for this? Her mother? Entrenched social norms?

While her own parents' marriage was not a traditionally arranged one, as they were living in the same village and knew each other before their parents organised the wedding, the same was not true for my mother. After she had to quit school her days were largely spent in the village weaving mattresses.She was considered by the villagers to be very beautiful, her hair long enough to sit on.

In late 1985, a young man not living on the island came to visit his cousin who lived near my mother's house. While he barely spoke a word to my mother, he took every opportunity he could to pass by her house to see her, as she was often sitting outside, under the house, weaving with her mother. It seemed as if he had fallen in love with her at first sight and while his interest was clearly apparent to my grandmother, my mother assured her she wasn't interested in return.

Around the same time, the commune chief also spied my mother as she was weaving, and decided that she would make a great wife for his 20 year-old son. He told my grandmother of his intentions, but she did not agree during this first meeting. He came back again a few days later.

She had been thinking seriously about his offer, as being a widow there was no man in the family to help earn money. If my mother got married there would then be a male family member to help her. So she made up her mind to accept the offer of marriage for her daughter, to a man she had not met.

My mother, of course, had no say in the matter. As a dutiful daughter she had to respect the decisions of her elders. Any concerns that she might have had about marrying an unknown man, and living with him for the rest of her life, were irrelevant in a cultural environment where young women had no voice.

She did not want to get married. She felt she was still too young, and not ready to become a wife, yet such reservations could not be voiced openly in a society that prioritized marriage for women as the only way that they could be supported in life. Having a husband, and soon after children, was the expected norm, not an option to be discussed.

In the eyes of her family and neighbours, as a 21 year-old she should certainly get married. Indeed she was one of the oldest unmarried women in the village. Having decided that her daughter should marry my grandmother gave her a choice – either marry the rice farmer who had come to visit his cousin and had shown so much interest in her, or accept the proposal from the commune chief for his son. She still didn't want to marry either of them but that choice was not one she had. She chose the man lived closer to her home and who could possibly offer her a more secure future.

My parents met for the first time on their wedding day. To make the situation even more uncomfortable it was a big service, as the commune chief was well known in the region and this was the first wedding among his sons. Over 1,000 people came to join in the dinner and dancing afterwards. Such a prestigious wedding was a clear sign of my mother's – and her mother's – new social standing in the community.

Despite this, my great grandmother was still opposed to the wedding, fearing that her granddaughter was marrying a provincial "dark-skinned guy," as my mother remembers it. To have dark skin in Cambodia is seen as sign that one is a rural farmer of Khmer ethnic roots, something the urbaine, often partially ethnically Chinese middle and upper classes have traditionally tried to distance themselves from.

A 20 year-old farmer who had had his marriage arranged by his father was clearly beneath any woman in my great grandmother's family, even if she had still not fully accepted my mother and grandmother into the family.

Yet the wedding went ahead, and they are still married to this day, but I have always questioned if love is possible in arranged marriages as I have never seen my parents hug each other, let alone kiss. It still makes me wonder if they have ever truly been in love. At the same time, the closeness of our family and the support they give to all of us, and each other, is clear to see.

My mother says that while she is unsure of the feelings I suggest she should be demonstrating, she deeply cares for my father. She says that she chose him, over the man from the other village, and how nervous she had been on her wedding day marrying an unseen man.

"And now you have three children with him," I tease her. "Yes! Wonderful children indeed," she always replies.

Sometimes such conversations can become a little awkward, as she seems reluctant to tell me certain things. I think my parents had to learn how to love each other, living and working together each day. They embarked on the same new journey together. This was aided by my father being a polite and quiet man she says, which meant they never argued.

She once told me that if she had had the same freedoms over her life as I do, that she wouldn't have married when she did, and she certainly would have continued her studies.

I know that her situation is not unique in Cambodia, or indeed elsewhere in the world. The lack of female leaders and role models in women's lives here meant they had few examples to inspire them to fight for the ability to live as they wanted. Not that the arranged marriage was easy on my father either. He had been planning to take the police entrance exams but had cancelled after his father told him of the wedding.

The contrast with my own life is great. When I was 21, the age my parents were when they were married, I was still at university. I was living my life how I wanted and was lucky enough to be travelling all over Europe in the free time from my exchange programme. I still find it hard to imagine my mother sitting under her house, weaving mattresses and preparing for her marriage, compared to what I was doing.

I am certain that I could never marry a man I have never met. In fact, I know I could never do it, because I have experienced full ownership of my life. But despite the lack of public affection my parents seem to have been able to live happy and fulfilling lives together, which I am very thankful for.

This is not to say they would not have prefered things differently, and I am sure they have both wished they had had more control in choosing who they married. Cultural stigma against divorce, especially in rural communities, would have made both their lives uncomfortable if they had remained in the village. A lack of state support for single mothers also meant that once my mother became pregnant with my eldest brother, it was virtually impossible that she could have charted any other course for her life.

However, both of them are very clear on one point. After their experiences of arranged marriage they will not subject their children to the same. Which is lucky, as arranged marriages are still prevalent in Cambodia and I have had to decline three such proposals from prospective parents-in-law seeking a wife for their sons.

The first was when I was 17 and still in high school. A family in my village wanted me to marry their son, who had quit school years before and worked alongside his father making rice wine.

When I was 19, a local wealthy family wanted me to marry their unruly son. I had heard that he was in a gang and that he spent lots of his mother's money. Why on earth would I want to marry him!

The last proposal was just as ridiculous as the other two. While I was studying in the Czech Republic, my mother called to tell me that her friend had asked if

I would marry her son. While we had once been neighbours I hadn't seen the family since I was two. Thankfully my mother said that she would ask me, and I of course declined.

I told my parents I would never accept an arranged marriage and they have respected my decision. I am very thankful that I have had the education, life experience and freedom to decide by myself, otherwise I would very likely have had to marry one of those men.

I have been an independent woman since I left my village after high school, and to a large extent I have done whatever my heart desired. I have the freedom to choose who I trust, be that a friend or a potential life partner.

I find it scary that in this day and age that such restrictive cultural traditions can still exist.

Chapter 5: A Single Parent

"Family is the safest place, and we could always return"

My father discussed with my mother about leaving for Pailin

I n 1992 my parents were not happy. I was two, and my brother Rithy five, and our family was finding it difficult to raise themselves up from the level of basic farmers.

More than 10 years after the fall of the Khmer Rouge the country had come a long way, but rural life was still very difficult. The country was still not fully safe, with pockets of armed resistance continuing to fight against the government and hindering easy travel and trade throughout Cambodia.

My parents were living the lives that seemed predetermined for them. After trying to operate a small ferry business to the mainland for the first three years of their marriage, with my father paddling people across the river at any time of day or night, they eventually returned to farming. My father grew rice and vegetables as my mother raised pigs around our house, and while we had enough food to eat meals were basic, and we had no luxuries.

As a way of making more money my father suggested moving to work in the gem mines of Pailin province, the same area where he had spent his final days as a child soldier. Pailin had long been a prosperous town because of its extensive gem deposits, and many people from all over the country travelled there with the hope of searching for gemstones and becoming rich.

People in our village had taken to commenting on our family's poverty, lacking as we did the motorbikes or gold jewellery that signified wealth in rural Cambodia. My father's desire to earn more money wasn't to buy such things, but rather to have enough money to ensure that we ate well, could attend school, and be as comfortable as possible.

He left us in March 1992 for Pailin, and just like that my mother effectively became a single mother, in charge not just of looking after the rice field and pigs but also two young children. Life was lonely and I cried each night asking for him to return.

With his departure, communication with him was effectively cut off. There was no working national telephone system and the postal service outside of the few major cities was still not running again. Fighting was still taking place across the country, with regular bombings and shootings even in areas deemed safe. Cambodia remained an unsafe place.

Nationwide transport had also not yet recovered, and "shared taxis" were often the only way to get around, with six or seven passengers often cramming into a tired old Toyota. This is how my father got to the northern city of Battambang, from where he walked for three days to get to Pailin town.

Upon arrival he discovered that his plans to earn enough money for the family had been widely out of touch with reality. Many other men had travelled there with similar dreams and competition to find gemstones was fierce. With no way to communicate with us about his situation and quickly accepting that gem hunting was a fruitless endeavor he decided to start selling vegetables to the miners instead. This proved equally as unprofitable, so he started to clear a patch of land about the size of a football pitch on which to grow his own produce to sell.

This was a very risky venture as much of the Cambodian border with Thailand was heavily mined. Known as the K-5 minefield, an untold number of anti-personnel mines were laid by the Vietnamese troops in the early 1980s in an effort to stop Khmer Rouge soldiers crossing back into the country from their Thai bases. Demining work along the border continues to this day.

While my father was risking life and limb in Pailin province my mother's life was no less challenging. She would be up at 4:30am each day to begin the farming tasks, and after feeding the pigs would set off on her bicycle to our rice field, some 6km and a ferry ride away. I would go with her sometimes, sitting in the basket on the front of the bike.

Alone, looking after children on the island much as her mother had done with her, she was sometimes afraid of her vulnerability. With no street lighting and little police patrolling, safety in the village was traditionally the responsibility of the men of the house. With no word from my father, she continued to do all of our farming tasks. Raising pigs was expensive, but offered the highest returns, and each time she sold one for slaughter she would go to buy gold and save it.

Meals were very simple, often just rice and two boiled eggs dipped in soya or fish sauce. To stop us complaining she would tell us that when the early Chinese settlers made their way to Cambodia – and as we were partially Chinese the story resonated – they had so little to eat that they had to eat the legs of the small crabs that live in the rice fields. Her tactic worked and my brother and I were grateful for whatever food we were given to eat.

Every night the village became very dark and quiet. With no cinema or entertainment to distract people, most people would go to bed shortly after eating dinner and locking the door.

I was still very young and would often cry for my father, which would cause my mother to quickly wake up and try to quiet me. She was concerned that my cries would alert any roaming thieves to that fact that my father was absent. Her fear was not without cause. In the absence of effective policing people in our village took care not to advertise any vulnerability they might have. I was oblivious to this of course.

In 1993, after a year of taking care of the family by herself, my father returned. He did not come back with gemstones or even money for the family, only with a severe case of malaria.

He was in a serious condition and with no medicine or doctors available nearby, my mother made the decision to take him to the Khmer-Soviet Hospital in Phnom Penh. I went with her to stay by him while he recovered.

In Cambodian hospitals, and especially in those days, family members usually sleep next to the patient and are often in charge of providing food. I can remember enjoying the breakfast of grilled pork and rice that my mother would buy for me as this was a luxury we didn't have at home.

It took him 10 days to recover, and the cost of treatment used up all the gold my mother had saved over the year he was away.

All I could think about was how good the food had been, and how different Phnom Penh was to where I lived. For me, the time in hospital had been great! While we had been there, Cambodia was preparing for the first national election for more than 20 years.

The United Nations had taken over the running of the country following the signing of the Paris Peace Accords in October 1991 which officially ended the war with Vietnam. These elections were supposed to mark the beginning of a new, peaceful Cambodia.

However, my parents were worried that the voting would again spark violence and so they decided it was safer to leave the capital and return to the relative safety of our island. Two days before voting was due to take place my father checked out of the hospital and we travelled home.

While the voting was in fact relatively peaceful, it did unfortunately not solve the violence in the country, which continued for another four years until the Khmer Rouge surrendered in 1998 shortly after the death of Pol Pot.

It took my father years to recover from his malaria. It is a very serious disease if left untreated and the time it had taken him to get to hospital had been almost too long. His slowly-improving condition meant that my mother had another person to look after. Her life was certainly tough, but she is an incredibly strong woman.

When he was recovered enough to walk around he started to help again on the farm, and was soon growing vegetables in addition to our rice field. The skills he had learnt cultivating vegetables for the last year finally payed off and for a number of years my mother ran a small grocery store to sell some of his surplus and other items needed in the village. Saving as much money as possible my father was able to buy a new Honda motorbike which meant he could travel between home and the fields more quickly, and further increase his productivity.

Business was growing and everything seemed to be going well. In November 1994 my brother Sela – meaning 'rock' – was born. He was a big baby and cried every evening until my father learnt to put him on the motorbike and slowly drive around the village. I was really proud to have a baby brother and he took our family up to five. We were finally together and feeling like a normal family.

Chapter 6: Growing Up In The 1990's

"Appreciate every little life experience and hardship, they make you a better person in the future"

I helped my parents carrying water from the river

I was born in 1989 in the house in which my mother had been born 24 years earlier, into a farming family on the small island of Koh Ksach Tunlea. The island, some 40km south of Phnom Penh, takes less than two hours to cycle around and is home to about 6,000 people.

Our isolated island only started to get government-installed running water and electricity in late 2014, and so carrying water from the river to be boiled for cooking and cleaning was a perpetual task for me as a child. Although we lived 400 meters from the water, I have always been small and would always have to make numerous trips to get enough.

Most people in the village still use wood for cooking, so collecting firewood was also a common task for me. I would go with some of the other girls who lived by my house. Often taking a snack of unripe mango with chilli and salt – very popular in Cambodia – we would spend hours searching for small branches. These we would tie into a small bundle and carry back on our heads, singing silly songs and sharing stories. Once home I would cut the branches into smaller pieces that were easier for cooking, and dry them in the sun. The yearly challenge was to collect enough in the dry season to last when the months-long rainy season arrived.

Most evenings it was my job to cook the rice for dinner as I waited for my parents to come back from the farm. While I had plenty of tasks, my brothers were also busy cutting grass to feed the cows we bought in 1997, or help with farming.

I have been always a headstrong girl. Much like my mother, if I was told something was not possible I would endeavour to do it. Sometimes I succeeded, but other times when I came up against entrenched gender bias it was harder as a young girl to challenge. I can remember my elder brother refusing to let me play football with him and his friends as he felt I should play girls games instead. I couldn't understand why girls and boys had such defined hobbies and tasks.

Living so close to the river, fish was a regular part of our diet. After a long day farming my father would grab his fishing net and spend an hour or so catching dinner for us. I would often "help" by holding the bucket where he stored any catches. I always found it a lot of fun, holding the fish and walking along the river bank but he must have been exhausted by this time each day and I am sure I just slowed things down.

His days were spent farming. As we did not have an irrigation system to carry pond water to the rice and vegetables he had to carry up to 100 bucket-loads each day to ensure they were properly watered.

My mother once told me that the only task I had to do for her was to study hard. I worked as hard as I could in the local school. I would go in the mornings, but due to a lack of teachers there were no classes in the afternoon so I would play with my friends and also try to earn money when I could.

By grade 4 I was collecting leaves from tamarind trees near my house to sell. Along with a neighbour – who was shunned by the village for being HIV positive, something she had been born with – we would pick up to 1.5kg of the leaves. We had no fear of climbing and I wondered if I was somehow like a monkey. Luckily we never fell.

We would then put the leaves into smaller 50g bags, which is how much is used as an ingredient in a popular sour soup recipe. I would earn $0.20 for 12 of the small bags and would have to paddle our neighbor's canoe across the river to the local market. On a good day I might get $0.80 for my efforts, which I gave to my parents to cover the cost of my schooling. Of course I didn't need to do this but I wanted to try to help them as they worked so hard and I was already developing a sense of independence.

I also sold vegetables from my parent's farm such as tomatoes, chinese broccoli, cabbage and snake beans. Anything that was left after my parents had collected the best vegetables I would put in a basket which sometimes weighed 8kg, and carry to the market to sell to local retailers. As I had spent nothing on growing the vegetables I was able to undercut the other sellers and I always sold out quickly. This venture proved to be much more profitable, and sometimes netted me $5.00.

I would keep some of the money and give the rest to my mother to help with buying food. I think by allowing me to go sell the vegetables and leaves they knew I would become more independent and gained valuable insights in trading and dealing with people. Earning the money was difficult and it made me realize how hard my parents worked to support our family. I tried to save as much as I could from every sale so that when I wanted to buy something for myself I would have enough money.

I learned the skill of negotiating with the vendors, and I learned how to persuade buyers to buy my products. I learned how to be patient because picking tamarind leaves one by one was not an easy job. Above all, I gained valuable survival skills in entrepreneurship.

Despite all of my efforts to make money, I do not think that my childhood was very different from the other children in my village. While they may have had more expensive toys to play with I had my own activities to entertain me. I spent much of my free time outside playing with my neighbours in the dirt and getting muddy when it rained. When I wasn't at school, playing or making money, I would follow my father as he went to search for crickets or frogs for us to eat. Life was simple.

My family may have worked hard to earn enough money to live on, but it taught my brothers and I to appreciate the time we had to play or explore. I feel bad for kids today in the city. Now that there is regular electricity they no longer have to seek out their own entertainment, but can just sit by themselves and play on computer games or waste time on Facebook, like children across the world.

In many ways, I am proud to have grown up during the 1990s because I gained so many valuable life experiences through the challenges I faced. I am not sure I would have had these had I been born later.

I earned money from picking tamarind leaves

My friends and I went to find the firewood for cooking

Chapter 7: Hard Work, Low Wages

*"Some people have so much
that they don't even realize how
privileged they are, but some still
struggle just to make a living"*

I was waiting for the boat to go home

In my parents' village most families continue to earn a living much as people here have always done, by going fishing, searching for snails or frogs, and farming. A simple life which is not to say that life is easy. Infact far from it. People spend most of their time working to earn enough money to feed their families.

As a child I was always busy finding ways to make money. From the age of 10 until I was 16 I would use a short school holiday in late March to go to harvest peanuts. Along with some of our neighbours I would cross onto the mainland and work as a labourer on a local peanut farm. With a packed lunch and long-sleeved clothes to protect me from the sun in what was the hottest time of the year, I would spend the days on large peanut farms.

My younger brother and other children his age would follow behind the older kids and adults as they picked up the nuts, collecting what we had missed. Working between 7am and midday, and again until 5pm, the days were long, hot and exhausting. There were usually 15 or 20 people working on each farm, and there was a feeling of haste in the harvest as it needed to be finished before the dry season ended and the rains arrived.

Each exhausting day I would earn about $1.75, and it didn't help that the farms were about 3km from the ferry back to our island.

Almost all the children in the area would go to pick peanuts to make some extra money. The village would be quiet as no one was around to play and make noise. The school holidays came just before the Khmer New Year, a very important annual holiday, and everyone, including children, wanted to have some money to enjoy the festivities.

When I was 13 I wanted a new pair of jeans and a shirt to wear to celebrate the new year, so I saved all my money from the peanut harvest. Over 15 days of working eight hours in the hot sun, I saved $30 and was able to get the clothes I wanted. While it was a lot of money for a 13 year-old child, it certainly hadn't been easy to earn, and I was exhausted.

My goal to make enough money that year also was not without some danger. Near the end of the harvest, after leaving the peanut farm following a long day of work I was a little behind the others walking home as I had wanted to try and find a few extra peanuts to give to my mother for dinner. However I lost track of time, and by the time I had returned to where the ferry would wait to take us back to our island everyone had already left. It was getting darker and everything was so quiet. This was before the island had electricity and I could only see one or two kerosene lanterns on the other bank.

I started to get a little nervous, and tried calling to an elderly man, named Louch, who lived near our house and would sometimes give me rides across the river in his boat. But despite calling his name, he didn't reply. After another 30 minutes or so, it slowly dawned on me that I was the only person on this side of the river waiting to cross, but I thought someone must eventually come by. An hour later and I was worried, as I didn't want to have to spend the whole night here. I wondered if my mother was scared that I had not been at home for dinner. Maybe she was trying to get people to come and find me?

After a further half hour I decided my only option was to swim home. It was dry season so the water level was low, and the distance was not far. So I borrowed an empty 30-litre plastic bottle from people on the mainland to give me something to hold onto, and started swimming.

I had never swum across the river before, and I managed to scare myself imagining there were crocodiles in the water, but somehow I made it across. Being surrounded by water most of the kids in the village learnt how to swim before they were 10, normally with some help from parents or older siblings. Drownings remain very high though, and I count myself very lucky to have swum across safely..

When I walked into the house, dripping wet, my mother was very angry that I had dared to swim, but she was happy I was home and safe. Eating my long-overdue dinner I was secretly proud of my achievement, the riskiest thing I had done in my life at that point, and something I will never forget!

Why did I go to such lengths to get $1.75, I have asked myself subsequently. It was just something I wanted to do. Even though earning money like this was very hard I enjoyed being as self-sufficient as possible and I really appreciated every bit of money I earnt.

It certainly taught me the lesson that hard work pays off eventually. It also taught me just how hard my parents worked to support themselves and my brothers and me. They never complained about their hard lives, and I have endeavoured to copy that attitude in my own life.

I also had the motivation to make the money as I wanted a new set of clothes for the upcoming holiday celebrations. Khmer New Year is the time when farmers have finished their harvests, and it is a time for celebration. Big feasts, new clothes, lots of cleaning, there is always a lot to do and prepare for, but it doesn't feel like work, as families come together and look forward to the upcoming year. It was always my favourite holiday.

This year though, having worked so hard to earn the money to buy new clothes, and risking the swim across the river, I was almost too shy to wear the new jeans and shirt. They were so new that I was concerned that I would stand out in my village, as my normal clothing was so simple. But I soon overcame this with the joy of eating so much good food, and seeing my extended family. The laughter, smiles, food and stories made the holiday as much fun as always, and my fears were forgotten.

Thinking back to those days, the amount I earned after working all day was less than rich people would pay for their breakfast in Phnom Penh. At the time I wondered if all my life would be so difficult, but I didn't have anything to compare it to. Everyone I knew worked very hard all day.

Chapter 8: Womanhood

"Young women deserve to learn about, and understand, what is going on with their body"

I passed my final primary school exam in 2001. Students had the choice of continuing their studies at Troysla secondary school on the east side of the island or Preah Sihanouk secondary school located on the west side.

I chose Preah Sihanouk school because they offered private language classes in English, Thai, and even Chinese, and this seemed like an exciting opportunity to learn something new. Everything about my new school was new, even though it wasn't too far away from my house. I had new friends, could study new subjects and was able to finally have a bicycle to ride the 5km to school and back each day.

The bike had been my older brother's and was a mountain bike, a rarity on the island where most people had traditional-style bikes with baskets and only one gear.

Even for my generation, after all of the changes that Cambodia had undergone and the development it had received, female education was given lesser importance to that of boys. My father's father questioned why I, aged 12, was still in school, and not working at a factory to make money for the family.

His lack of support for my education was very painful, but rather than sulk and feel down I was determined to just study even harder and prove him wrong about the value of my education. Thankfully my parents supported me, believing that all their children – whether boy or girl – should finish secondary school.

My excitement about studying English was probably rather strange on our rural island, but I knew that it would help me in the future, and ensure that I wouldn't be a garment factory worker
as my grandfather had encouraged.

My form teacher was young and new to her job, and the energy she brought to Khmer literacy, English and morality lessons meant they were my favourite subjects. She made me want to become a teacher as well. English was an extra subject which I took for an hour each day at noon. I was worried that students who lived closer to school would learn it quicker than me as they would have more time to study; due to the distance I had to travel I was unable to make the evening class as well. Everyone warned me that it was not safe for a young girl to be out after dark, that bad men would try to rape me, and that fear was enough to limit my lessons just to lunch time.

The classes cost 200 riel ($0.05) an hour, and we slowly worked through the level one textbook. My teacher was called Ms. Laiheang. She had the most beautiful and gentle voice, and I could sit and listen to her for hours.

Three times a week I would help my parents by carrying up to 15 kg of guava on my bike to sell to a dealer at school. They paid 10 cents per kilo, and this was one way that my parents paid for my education. Some of the kids made fun of me for doing this, saying it was old fashioned and poor, but I did not care as I was able to study!

I was very shy, and focused as much as possible on my studies, and helping my parents with the farm and chores in my free time. Twelve years old, I had no interest in talking to boys other than my brothers-but my mother still warned me not to do anything that might cause people to gossip about me or the family – such as have a boyfriend.

Despite my trips to the market to sell vegetables, or to pick peanuts, I still lived a very sheltered existence. My perspective on life did not extend much beyond the island. I didn't have the internet with which to learn more about the world and our family only had an old black and white television that did not really help as I was only allowed to watch cartoons, mainly Tom and Jerry.

One day during my first year at secondary school, as I was cycling to the farm to have lunch with my mother and brother, I noticed a dark wet patch on my navy blue skirt, and blood on my saddle. I stopped the bike in panic. I had no idea why I was bleeding or what was wrong with me. Even by the age of 12 no one had told me anything about my body and the changes that would take place as I grew older. Reproductive health was not something taught at school, and parents were often unable or unwilling to talk openly about such things.

I made my way to the farm and in tears went straight to my mother and showed her the blood and asked her what was wrong with me.

Calmly, patting my head to sooth me, she said that this was perfectly normal and that I would be fine. She explained that my period had started, the first time I had ever heard the word, and she then proceeded to tell me everything she knew. She told me that it comes every month, and might last up to a week, that any pains normally happen in the first few days but is usually short but sometimes very uncomfortable. All of this was new to me.

While I was no longer scared, I was still confused and rather nervous about what this would mean for my life from now on. Would I still be able to run and play as before? Why had she not told me about this before?

My mother went to my aunt's house, which was nearby, and asked my cousin for a sanitary pad. She returned with something in a black plastic bag, as if it was not meant to be seen in public. She taught me what it was for, and showed me how to use it. Then she gave me a warning. From now on, she said, I was not a little girl any more, and I had to be careful. I still remember what she said next.

"Be careful not to let any boys touch you, you could get pregnant."

What ghastly facts to divulge to a 12-year-old girl who was already too shy to talk to boys!

I believed her for about a year until I was finally taught about human reproduction in grade 8, and was given more practical advice on avoiding unwanted pregnancy. The science behind pregnancy, how sperm and eggs meet to form a human being was fascinating to learn, and I felt a little silly that I had believed what my mother had told me.

The boys in class found it all funny, but for us girls, brought up to be quiet and respectful, it caused many to blush. I never talked about this topic with my brothers at all. They did not bother to ask either.

Access to clear information about such important issues about female health is still something that is not openly discussed in Cambodia. Women may discuss things amongst themselves, but public discussion on health and safe sex for example, is still considered taboo, especially in rural areas.

Chapter 9: The Thunder Storm

*"When life gives you a hard time,
don't give up, it is just a test"*

It was Sunday in the rainy season and I was helping my mother cut grass for the cows. The year was 2004, and my father was working in Phnom Penh as a supervisor on construction sites, coming home twice a month to visit us. My older brother was also in Phnom Penh studying English Literature at university, and staying at the Toul Tom Pong pagoda with the monks. Only my mother, younger brother and I were living at our house on the island.

As before, my mother was once again singlehandedly handling the dual duties of being a mother in charge of children and working on the farm. In addition to growing vegetables and rice, since 2000 we had now expanded to growing guava, and had almost 500 trees on a small adjacent plot. We were able to harvest fruit, which my younger brother and I loved, normally twice a week and could often collect 1.2 tons a month, netting us about $120. This money went to pay for my older brother's university costs, with the rest helping to cover my and younger brother's schooling.

In order to get enough food for our three cows a lot of grass had to be collected from all over the island, which we would transport home on our small boat. I didn't enjoy the job and my technique with the small scythe used to cut the grass was terrible. I often ended up cutting myself. It was sweaty work but I had to help my mother and I still have a scar on my hand reminding me of this time. Whenever I look at the mark on my little finger, memories flood back. It reminds me of the challenges I have faced in life and the lessons I learnt during my childhood.

My morning routine at this time first involved tying up the cows in the field near our farm where they could find grass for themselves. The two adult cows I would separate a little, so they would get enough grass each, while the baby was allowed to wander freely. He was a beautiful light-orange colour and never went far as he was still drinking his mother's milk. After I had done this, I would go back to help my mother cut more grass for them for the evening when they were tied up by our house. Once we had enough, this would be put in old rice bags, which made it easier to carry home.

Most afternoons during the rainy season it rains, and on this day the sky was getting increasingly darker as grey clouds started to build into a threatening mass above us. Approaching thunder sounded like the drums the monks at the nearby pagoda beat to summon their fellows for evening meditation – loud and steady. Lightning cut through the sky in great bursts of light. The wind had started to gust and whip up dust that stung my eyes and face. I was scared. This rainstorm was much angrier than any I could remember before, and it was accompanied by a strange smell, different to normal rain, which only added to my sense of dread.

The strong wind started to blow and shake the trees. The people near my farm, started to run and hide into their home. There was almost nobody was out, except my mother and I. We were still outside trying toone get back to the house as soon as we could, though our house was on the other side of the lake.

Acting calmly, my mother picked up the rice bags full of grass, closed the gate to the farm, and starting slowly running towards our house, dragging the two adult cows by their ropes with the baby following. I had my own bag to carry, but I was terrified and I was shaking like a lost baby bird out of its nest. The wind was now so strong that it felt like it would pick me up into the air and blow me away.

My mother was now moving so fast that it looked like her feet were not touching the ground but somehow I kept up with her. We were soaked to the skin the instant the rain started. My little brother, who was nine, was home alone at this time and so my mother had the added fear of his safety on her mind. Our old house was not strong and the storm seemed like it might blow it down with him inside.

Most people used small boats to cross the small lake by our house, but we had to take the cows home and so were walking across. The water was as high as my chest, and it slowed me a lot, making me more scared. I was crying as I struggled to get home and hide from the rest of the storm, and my mother did her best to motivate me to keep moving.

I knew she must have been scared as well, but she was strong and her motivation worked. Thirty minutes after I had first noticed the storm we arrived home, safe but exhausted. My mother found my brother hiding in his bed with a look of total fear on his face. He complained that he had been alone but we were all thankful to be together again and safe.

An hour later, and the storm had passed. Everywhere was soaked, and branches and litter was strewn across the village. After the noise of the wind and thunder, only the sound of thousands of frogs seemingly crying for more rain could be heard.

From the house I could see people slowly venturing outside, children trying to catch the frogs and adults getting food for their dinner. It reminded me how hungry I was, and just like that, my fear of the storm had left.

This childhood memory has stayed with me clearly. As well as showing rural life in Cambodia I think it clearly demonstrates the fact that after a scary or troubling event, so long as we do not give up, sooner or later life will get better again. The storm will pass.

Chapter 10: That Thing Called 'Education'

"Parents will gladly exchange all their hard work and sweat for a good education for their children"

I biked 14 kilometers both to and back from school everyday

I first started attending school when I was four. According to my mother, this was to ensure that I became familiar with education as soon as possible, and hopefully also make friends.

I spent grade one at Portivong Primary School, which is where my mother had gone after she was able to restart her studies in 1979. My first class was at the beginning of October 1994, and it was only a five minute walk to the small wooden schoolhouse, next to the 'new' pagoda. Calling it 'new' is funny as it was still old, just newer than the other nearest pagoda in the next village.

Each morning, my five year-old cousin Bros and I would walk to school, where I would spend the 100 riel ($0.03) note mother had given me to buy a breakfast snack of rice soup and a small piece of bread. The bell would ring at 7am and everyone was supposed to go to class, but we rarely actually went, rather just ate the soup and then went home to play all day. As we never got in trouble, I guess our parents did not mind.

A year later, and things were a bit different. This time I had to attend, so no more soup and then going home. In fact I went so far as to sit at the front of the class, right next to the teacher, and this time I stayed long enough to make some friends.

As the smallest girl in my class, I was sometimes picked on by some of the other girls. One, Sophal, was taller than everyone else, and took the role of the class bully. I can not remember what caused her to scratch my face one day, but it has left a scar to this day. An unfortunate memory of a nasty classmate.

My mother told me to focus on my studies instead of worrying about the other girls. The combination of my love of learning and her nightly help with my homework meant I was always better prepared for class each day than everyone else. Because of my playful first year avoiding school however, I had to spend seven years in primary school, rather than the usual six.

At the time, French was the official foreign language that had to be taught at school. Lessons started in grade 5. My teacher was very strict, hitting children if they made mistakes, and this old fashioned idea that fear is a good motivator actually hindered my French studies. I really did not enjoy the classes. I remember once getting less than 40 percent in a test and my teacher hitting my hand with a big wooden ruler. After four strikes, I had a deep blue bruise that stayed for a week. I was scared to make any mistakes, rather than motivated to enjoy studying. I couldn't understand why they thought mistakes were so bad as my parents had told me that making mistakes were an important part of learning. People always make mistakes. It is natural because no one is perfect.

Yet despite my terrible French classes, I was reminded daily how lucky I was to be going to school at all. A few of my neighbours whose parents were uneducated, and therefore did not appreciate the value in sending their children to school, instead had their children help them at their farms all day.

It was difficult to grow up around such an environment in which education was not always respected. I am so glad my parents were different, but the local authorities also seemed to feel education was not very important. There were not enough teachers at my school, so I was only able to study in the morning – another group of students would study in the afternoon – and there certainly were not enough books.

Most parents just wanted their children to be able to read and write to a basic level before they would take them out of school to help with family businesses. This was very different to my own parent's plans for their children, which involved expanding our horizons through education as much as possible.

By secondary school my daily lessons cost 800 riel, which is still less than $0.20, but felt like a lot of money for my family, especially as there were three of us in full time education. The lack of teachers had barely improved by that point as well and I would go to school for only three full days a week.

In Cambodia, secondary school is only three years, from grades 7 to 9. At this point students willing and able must take an exam to enter high school. I say this because by the end of grade 9, many of my female classmates had already dropped out of school, usually to work to support their family, and most had had no say in the decision. This was normally for financial reasons and if a family could only afford to send one child to school, their first priority would almost always go to a son.

The distance to the nearest high school was also off-putting for some of my classmates. I had to cycle a 14-km round trip to get to class each day, in addition to taking a ferry off the island, and this had to be done throughout the rainy season, when roads were little more than giant muddy puddles.

In 2004, the same year as the memorable thunderstorm, my older brother moved to Phnom Penh for university, I was just starting high school, and my younger brother was still in secondary school. My father was working in Phnom Penh on construction sites and so my mother had to deal with a lot of work in addition to the full time task of managing our farm. To top it off, our family's financial situation, not helped by having three kids in education, meant that money was very tight and she often skipped meals to ensure we could continue our studies. This would unfortunately lead her to suffer from ulcers a few years later.

My older brother's costs were the highest as he was living in the capital and university is not free in Cambodia. My costs were not insignificant either, as I was taking extra lessons in addition to the normal school classes. Due to the lack of funding, resources and teachers at school, my chances of passing the high school exams were very slim without the additional help. As passing high school is the requirement for me to go to university, I knew I needed to study more, and that meant taking the same private lessons that my older brother had required.

So every weekday morning, I had to wake up at 4:30am to cook rice and either a boiled egg or an omelette to take for my lunch. Like any teenager around the world, waking up so early was the last thing I wanted to do, and it felt as if my eyes were only half open as I prepared each morning.

Almost every day I wished that I did not have to be up so early making my lunch. I wished that I could be that child who was sent off to school by her parents with everything all done, or even better taken to school so I did not have to cycle so far. But of course that was not possible. If I wanted to pass high school and go to university, I knew I had to overcome the obstacles in my way. To achieve my dreams I knew I had to be up early, making the food that would give me the energy to study. Lying in bed was not going to allow me to do anything more than stay in the village, and this understanding really motivated me.

At this time of the day everything was still pitch black and quiet, with even the animals still asleep. Ghost stories are popular in rural Cambodia and most people believe in spirits to some extent – I certainly did at that age. Alone in the dark, it was scary and I was always on edge waiting for a ghost to appear.

Squatting in front of the little clay stove behind the house, with only a lantern for company, I would hear the village roosters make their daily call to announce the new day. After packing up my lunch, I would quickly dress into my uniform of white shirt and long blue skirt, and grab the old bicycle to start my journey to school through the still dark village. What an adventure to get that thing called education!

After two years of this daily routine I had made it to the final year of school at the age of 16. It was by far the hardest academic year of my life up to that point, and I rarely saw my parents. Between their hard work on the farm, and my many hours of extra lessons in addition to my normal studies, we really only interacted on Sundays.

Following my shy early years, by this stage I had been able to make a number of good friends who shared similar values as me: a love of education, a respect for their parents hard work, dreams of a future beyond our rural villages and an attitude of never giving up.

It was during this year that I first met an American named Charles Dibella. He was exploring Cambodia by bicycle and had started talking to my older brother in Phnom Penh. He decided he wanted to visit our village, and he became the first native English speaker I talked with. I was incredibly shy, but the experience was very motivating as it proved that this language I was learning was indeed a gateway to communicating with people from other countries. He has stayed in Cambodia and we have remained friends, and I often seek his advice on many things.

More immediate problems were our family's monetary poverty. My mother would often explain how little money we had, but stressed the need to be grateful for the important things in life, and to study hard, and this advice had stayed with me. It still does today.

Knowing the financial difficulties my parents worked so hard to overcome, I felt guilty each day taking the money from my mother to cover school costs. But her sacrifices to ensure my brothers and I could study were very inspiring, especially in my later high school years when I was better able to understand and appreciate them. If she would go hungry so that we could go to school, it must clearly be very important to her, and for us as well.

My entrepreneurial spirit had not left me, even as my school load had increased, and I always looked for ways to try to pay for my own studies. In high school, if classes finished early, I would buy around 12 small watermelons near the school, where they were cheaper than where I lived, and cycle with them back to my village. There I could make $0.10 profit on each one and earn enough in one trip to pay for two days of high school.

Not everyone at school had the same humble upbringing as me. In fact, I was one of the poorest children in my class, and I stood out because of it. Unlike those from richer families, I only had two dresses and shirts to last me for the academic year, and of course I had to cycle to class and eat the meager lunch I had cooked myself.

I was lucky enough to be helped by my English teacher Som Ol. Instead of the $10.00 he normally charged for 40 hours of private lessons, I only had to pay $5.00, which was just about affordable. It helped solidify my love of English and I have enjoyed writing in the language since then, as you can see!

His were not the only extra lessons I had to take. The facilities at our school were so basic that I needed extra classes in almost every subject to stand a chance of doing well in my final exams. This is the problem with education in many parts of Cambodia. The focus is not on having students truly understand the subjects, but rather just memorizing facts. I know this is a common complaint about education across the world, but in rich countries that are turning to this method, it has been a conscious decision, which I think is a mistake. In Cambodia however, classes are taught like this because schools lack the resources to do anything different, and teachers often do not have the experience or training to teach in any other way.

Another long-standing problem in Cambodia, but since government efforts starting in 2014 has greatly diminished, is that of cheating in tests. For richer kids it was very easy to bribe teachers or fellow students to help them pass tests, including the important national grade 12 exams. Coming from such a poor family, I had no option to cheat even if I had wanted to, and I was happy to spend what little money we could spare on my extra classes. That way I was actually learning, rather than just attending school to receive a graduation certificate.

This attitude of just bribing teachers to pass tests stems in part from the historically low salaries paid to teachers. It is only in 2016 that high school teachers base salaries have risen above $200 a month. While this is still better than farmers and garment factory workers, given the importance of teachers' roles in developing Cambodia's future workers and leaders it is a small amount of money. Such low salaries for low-level public servants has created a culture where the rich can bribe their way through school, into jobs, or out of traffic offenses or even court cases. I feel this has been detrimental to the country's economic and human resource development, and I am glad that I did not support that system as a student.

With the traditional role of women as being under-educated and left at home, this culture of bribery has also helped to cement the role of men in positions of authority. In a country where money can buy you anything, those with money have power, and that usually means men.

In many communities this has further entrenched the view that girls are not as valuable as boys, and are to be appreciated only for their beauty or domestic skills. This lack of appreciation contributes to girls being forced to drop out of school, the stubborn prevalence of arranged marriages, and for many becoming mothers early and being trapped in similar lives as their own mothers.

I wonder when the day will come when women in Cambodia are valued as equal to men? When will our level of education, our professional opportunities and salary expectations, and just basic respect not be on a different level?

I strongly believe, and I know I am not alone in this, that education forms a major part in bringing about this equality. It has the power not only to change individual lives, but whole societies as well.

I appreciate how lucky I have been in being supported by family and teachers to reach a level of education that is still not the norm in Cambodia. I did not have to leave school early to work on a farm or in a garment factory like many girls in my village. My dreams of a different life were kept within my control, and supported not hindered by those around me.

I did not need the fancy clothes and toys that my classmates placed so much importance in, and helped me further appreciate the sacrifices my parents made to even allow me to go to school, to provide for a more reliable education for their children.

Chapter 11: The 5,000 Riel Note

"Help those who really need the support; don't wait until afterwards when they don't need your help anymore"

Grandmother Sru gave me a 5,000 riel note for schooling

I might be hard to imagine that a 5,000 riel note could change one girl's life. At just $1.25, it buys breakfast in Phnom Penh, or maybe a small ice cream in Europe, but 10 years ago 5,000 riel was enough to keep me in high school for two days.

In my mind, I never had an image of myself quitting school to work in a factory. Instead, some days I would imagine I was on an airplane flying somewhere new, or in a university class, or exploring an exotic country. The problem with such dreams was that I knew they were reliant on my finishing high school, and that meant not just daily study, but daily extra classes as well.

My grandfather's cousin, Sru, lives near my parent's house. She is a small, a very thin old grandmotherly figure, who never attended school. I think that is why she took such care and attention of my brothers and I. She was always excited to see us in our uniforms. As a relative of my mother's, she also offered her emotional support in harder times, and occasionally financially too.

I can clearly remember one dark morning, when I was in grade 12, Sru walking over to our house and handing me a 5,000 riel note. It was not much money, she explained, but she wanted to help my studies, and hoped that this would assist me in becoming successful.

While the money was indeed helpful, allowing me two days of school and saving me from having to sell watermelons for a few days, what was more important to me was the clear signal her donation sent in terms of her support for me. She wanted me to succeed, and that meant more than the money.

I told her that when I was older, I would pay her back 100 times what she gave me. She smiled politely but I don't think she believed me, before explaining how difficult her life had been been, exacerbated by the fact that she had never been to school. She had many questions about the world around her, but no way to get answers, and she wanted to ensure that I was never in the same situation.

She also offered her help to us at home. When my parents were working in the field, she would sometimes drop by to check that we were ok and had food to eat, and she was often a guest at our house after dinner, talking with my mother and offering her whatever advice or support was needed.

The level of compassion she showed to our family meant I grew up thinking of her as my grandmother, and she was one of my favourite people in the village. Her kindness was in stark contrast to my actual grandparents, and the other relatives on my father's side, who offered almost no support for our family. Indeed, they actively tried to persuade my parents to make me drop out of school. They could not see beyond short term financial needs, and could not understand the value of the long-term investment in education.

I always remember those who have helped to lift me up when I have been down. People's good deeds take a more important place in my memory that those with opposing attitudes, but, of course, I have learnt from those experiences too. I am a stronger person today because of them.

Throughout my life I have been used to being looked down upon because of my poor, rural background, but I have never let that depress me. I prefer to be judged by my actions, and in that regard I know I am doing well.

Four years after Sru gave me the 5,000 riel note, I was able to repay her from my first real paycheck. I could only spare 40,000 riel ($10) but I was very happy to give it to her.

With tears in her eyes she graciously accepted the money, never expecting that the comment of a teenager would hold true. The next year, I was able to give her another 40,000 riel, and I was happy to have made a small difference in her life in return for the role her gift had played in mine.

What I find most amazing about this story is that she, an uneducated woman, better understood the value of education than some of my real family members. Whenever I return to the village to visit my parents, I make sure I visit Sru. She loves to hear stories of my life and travels, and is always amazed at how different my life is to her own and other women in the area. She is happy that she is part of my ongoing journey.

In life I have learned that it is important to help those who are in need, and it will probably be repaid when you need help yourself. Although Sru's financial help was very small, it was just what I needed at the time and the support it conferred was worth much more. She inspired me to share what I can with people in need, whether it is money, food, knowledge or just a hug – and to do so with joy.

After years, I gave grandmother Sru back my first $10. She was tearing up with joy

Chapter 12: Pursuing Higher Education

"Seeking a better life for the future"

I was the only female student in the classroom

Grade 12, the final year of school in Cambodia, was incredibly difficult for me and not just because of the pressure to study and pass the end-of-year exams.

A few months before the exam I became very sick. The local hospital did not know what was wrong with me, and so my mother took me to a hospital in Phnom Penh. I was worried that this would mean I would be unable to take the exams, and she told me it was ok to miss them this year, but I refused to consider her suggestion. I had to pass high school this year, I had worked so hard for so many years to reach this point!

The exam was to be held over two days in July, 2007. It consisted of 11 subjects, including English. The night before the exams were due to start I still had a strong fever and was incredibly stressed that I would not graduate this year. Through sheer perseverance I made it to the exam hall in Takmao town to take the exam the next morning, but despite doing the best I could I only received an E grade. In Cambodia this is still a pass, but I was so disappointed I cried for hours after learning my result a few weeks later.

While I had achieved my goal of passing high school, the result was too bad to secure any scholarship to help with university costs, and meant that my parents and I would continue to have to pay for my education.

It took me about two months to fully come to terms with my grade, and to move on. I had successfully graduated high school and that was the most important thing. My dreams were still ahead of me and I knew I could not end them all now. During boring school classes, or on my long bicycle ride to and from school, I had dreamt of leaving the village, of flying over our house, of writing books that people loved to read. It did not matter to me if other people thought that I was living in a fantasy world, and I had no expectations that these dreams would happen – but they did.

First step was to attend university, and that meant moving to Phnom Penh. I was nervous about living away from my family for the first time, in a city that offers a stark contrast to rural Cambodia. Other than my brief hospital stay a few months before, I had barely visited the capital, and did not know my way around at all.

My brother Rithy, who had spent two years in Phnom Penh for his own university studies, helped me and a female friend from my high school find somewhere to stay. We barely had any money and we were unable to stay with the monks as my brother had due to their celibacy rules, but we were lucky enough to find somewhere central for $20 each a month.

I arrived in October 2007 with my father, my new roommate and her father to make sure we settled in. I had left the village with a large smile on my face but a mixture of confused feelings. The life I was used to would never be the same again.

For starters, my new home was a great shock. It was tiny, and felt more like a shed for animals, rather than humans. Four first floor rooms in a row were connected via a walkway too narrow for two people to pass. There were no windows and it was always dark. The bathroom was outside. All I had was a cave-like room barely two meters wide.

In the two rooms next to ours lived women who worked at a Karaoke parlour, or KTV as they are commonly called. They would work for 4pm to 11:30pm and then sleep much of the day, and so would not only wake us up when they returned, but meant we had to be as quiet as mice during the day as well.

To go to use the toilet, we had to go downstairs and into a building next door, which housed a few male students and two families. Showering or washing clothes also took place in this shared space, and it always felt as if there were watching eyes. I did not feel secure, and my experience of living in this environment was a great shock.

For food, my friend and I had to light a small gas stove in the little space we had in our room, boiling water carried from the well downstairs. Everything was in such contrast to the space, the privacy and the relative comfort of the village.

Our room now became everything for us, including our library and living room. It was incredibly claustrophobic and I was reminded that even when our cows at home were locked up for the night they had more room to move around, and more comfort. We shared one mattress covering the wooden floor to sleep, but managed to hear the footsteps and conversation of our neighbors
through the thin walls; crying babies and arguing couples would keep us awake and we missed home, but we both knew we were lucky to be able to study.

It was not all bad, with the nighttime lights illuminating the beautiful architecture of the city reminding me of fireflies gathering in mangroves. The shopping malls, restaurants and entertainment centers were unlike anything we had seen before, and for many people they must have given the appearance that Phnom Penh was a veritable paradise.

However, my impression of the first day in Phnom Penh was not a positive one. Whereas in the village if I wanted food I could just go to the river to catch fish, or into the fields to look for snails, here everything had a price, and often a very steep one. There were too many people, and the traffic and pollution caused by the number of cars made cycling very difficult. It is now some 10 years later and things have only become worse!

It did not help that I was still unsure what to study at university. Most of the people I knew chose to study the popular courses like finance or banking, in the hope that after graduating they could work in the growing number of banks opening up across the country. An air conditioned office, smart clothes and a comfortable life lay ahead, but I had no such professional goal.

For reasons that I still cannot quite remember I decided to study information technology. In my class of over 30 students at the private Build Bright University I was the only female. I had no knowledge of computers at all and certainly did not have my own on which to practice and work. Whilst some of my classmates were friendly to me, being the only girl motivated me to prove to those who were less friendly that I was meant to be in this class.

As I had at primary, secondary and high school, I sat at the front of the class near the teachers, and tried to absorb all of the information they told me. But I felt isolated, as even my teachers were all male.

A few of the students from wealthier families brought in laptops to class to practice, play games and show off. Compared to what is available today these were huge, heavy lumps of grey plastic, but at the time they were cutting-edge technology in Cambodia.

Lacking this ability to freely practice what we were being taught, I told myself that by trying harder than everyone else I could keep up. I was forced to use the computer lab at university, which was small and had outdated equipment, but there was no way my parents could afford $500 for a computer for me on top of school fees and my other expenses.

Nor could they afford a motorbike or the expensive clothes that many of my classmates had. Instead, they bought me a dark red bicycle and I had to make do. While I knew at the time how silly it was to feel judged by things as insignificant as objects, I still stood out as not just the only girl, but also the poorest in class.

As I had before, I was keen to try to earn my own money to pay for as much of my studies as possible, but as a rural 17-year-old still getting lost everywhere I cycled, my chances of finding a job were much more difficult than at home; I couldn't transport watermelons to make profit, or harvest peanuts, sell vegetables or collect tamarind leaves as I had done previously.

I focused instead on my studies and grappling with the baffling world of computers. Slowly I began to recognize the street names and numbers and developed the confidence to cross the busiest ones. I was still a country girl, but I was adjusting to this new city and my new life.

After having been in Phnom Penh for about seven months, I found it easier to get around the city. It was about this time that my older brother introduced me to an NGO named "Protect the Earth, Protect Yourself," or PEPY. At the time they were working in Siem Reap province, helping to improve access to primary and secondary education in Krolanh district.

They were looking for an assistant to help in the afternoons in their Phnom Penh office, and it was at the interview that I met PEPY director Daniela Papi, a tall American with a big smile and a kind heart.

I got the job as a part-time translator and office assistant, and through this I met many interesting volunteers who came to Cambodia from around the world to volunteer. With a salary of $40 a month I felt like a queen! It was so much more money than I had earned during my leaf collecting or vegetable selling schemes as a child. Of course, this money I spent on my housing and food costs, not on pointless things, and I was once again able to help to reduce the financial burden of my studies on my parents.

By the end of 2008, Daniella decided to move PEPY closer to area where they were working, and as I wanted to continue to work for them, that meant I had to move as well.

Luckily, my university had a campus in Siem Reap city, so that part was straightforward, but convincing my mother to let me move so far from home was a more difficult feat. Phnom Penh was the furthest I had travelled up to this point, some two hours from my house, but Siem Reap in those days was a full day's journey.

Daniela spoke with my mother, and allayed her fears enough to grant me her permission, and along with my bicycle was soon living in the town famous for the nearby temple of Angkor Wat. With less traffic and more tourists with which to practice English, it was also a more pleasurable experience, even if I was once again the only female in my university class. As in Phnom Penh, I was sharing a room, but this time with Daniela. She was always very kind and respectful and she quickly became my role model, and friend.

Daniela is a hard working woman and along with my mother and grandmother, I set them as my examples for what it means to be a strong and independent woman.

As something of a big sister to me, she still offers support and guidance when I need it, and these are qualities I still believe are most important in a leader.

I believe that regardless of age, gender, or where we are from, having at least one good role model is very important. When we are young and forming our opinions of ourselves, having someone nearby who can inspire us to have confidence and do better in life is a very valuable gift. Daniela and the other great people I met at PEPY have helped to shape me into the person I am today, and for that I will forever be grateful.

Chapter 13: Settling In A New World

"True education is a magic spell that is able to change someone's life"

I was enjoying seeing the falling leaves of autumn for the first time in my life

When I was six I asked my father how airplanes could be so small and yet carry many people. The ones flying high over our farm looked tiny, and I had never seen one up close to see their true size. He tried to explain that they were so small because they were so far away, but I did not really believe him.

While it may not have lead to an understanding of visual perspective, it did spark within me an interest in flying, and from then on I often dreamed about taking airplanes to different, unknown places. For years afterwards, when I would hear the distinctive rumble of an airplane flying overhead I would look up until I could no longer see it. My dreams of travel had been awakened.

And once awakened, they have burned like fire within me every day since. When my mind would wander during class or in a quiet moment, I would imagine myself taking an airplane to explore somewhere new. The world I lived in was pretty small, and I knew almost everyone in my village and many people in my part of the island. This was of course comforting and friendly, but I yearned to get out, to see a world other than my own.

My lack of relatives outside of the island, let alone the country, my basic grasp of English and my family's relative poverty did not dampen this dream. Few people in my village had seen an airplane up close, and certainly never flown in one, and there were few books or television shows with which to satisfy my thoughts of travel. For most people, their vision did not extend much beyond the length of their rice field, and almost certainly not outside of Cambodia.

This is especially true of the females in my village, and in similar villages across rural Cambodia. Fantasies for many, until very recently, may have been limited to what type of husband they would be married off to. The traditional role of women in Cambodia as someone to just stay at home and support the family has been successfully re-enforced with a lack of access and support for education.

It is through my own education that I have been able to break free of these ties, and I hope that more and more girls can do the same. I was able to not just leave my village, or even my country, but to explore a whole new continent filled with excitement and unimagined wonders that outdid many of my childhood dreams.

None of this was easy of course. The shock of moving to Phnom Penh was great enough for me to deal with, and it took me a long time to adjust to the new people, environment and traffic. The news in June 2009 that I had been accepted on a full scholarship to study in the Czech Republic for three years was a surprise beyond words. I had applied almost on a whim, and did not expect to be offered the place, which required two years of IT experience and passing both a written test and face-to-face interview. Of 58 applicants, only two had been chosen.

If I thought the shock had been great for me, my mother's was even greater. She thought I might have inadvertently agreed to be trafficked, as she had seen enough films to know that the international trafficking of young women was a problem – and it is a present issue in Cambodia – and her imagination ran wild with possible gruesome scenarios.

I could hardly blame her for this, as I certainly did not understand where I was going or what I would experience. She had not travelled much further than Phnom Penh in her life, and to imagine her daughter flying halfway across the world for three years took her a long time to get used to. At the airport before my departure she was crying uncontrollably, and I hardly had dry eyes myself, but as I took my seat on the airplane I will filled with excitement. I was also able to appreciate for the first time just how big airplanes were, and my childhood of staring at them flying overhead flooded back.

The whole journey was one new experience after another for me. I had had to get a passport especially for the journey, and such things as metal detectors and passport control seemed very strange. This was also the first time I had had to function entirely in English for an extended period, and airport transfers and finding my gates all proved exhausting. All this before I had even arrived in the Czech Republic, which had a language and culture I knew nothing of.

The trip took 28 hours. Stepping out of the customs section at Prague airport I was very nervous, and everyone looked so strange. Tall white people, with blonde, brown or red hair, all dressed far differently to myself and walking very quickly. I felt like a tiny Cambodian girl in a different world.

I could not read any of the signs, even vending machines, which were a recent addition to my world in Cambodia, were again a mystery to me. I felt lost in this modernity.

Thankfully I was met by my new host family, who made the experience less scary and would help me quickly settle into my new life. It wasn't difficult for them to spot me, looking lost and feeling very cold, their instant warmth was calming, even if their kissing me instead of the palms-together bow I was more used to presented a surprising culture shock.

"Welcome to the Czech Republic, you've got a family here!" they said as we walked towards their car. Jacob drove, while his mother Eva sat in the front. Luba, a woman in her 60s and who was my host mother sat next to me, and her daughter Valerie – who I had met in Cambodia for my interview – sat on my other side.

It was autumn, and the view from the car window during the almost two-hour journey was filled with the most amazing golden and red leaves. This was my first experience of seasons other than Cambodia's 'wet' and 'dry', and I couldn't help but think I was dreaming. I kept looking for signs for the town of Hradec Kralove, my home for the next three years, but was largely mesmerized by the beautiful trees.

Although I had a host family, I actually lived in the Palachova student dormitories. There were eight, seven-story buildings, and I had been placed with a Mongolian room mate. Three girls shared a kitchen, and we had so much more space than the tiny cave-like room I was used to in Phnom Penh, and I especially enjoyed the big windows from which to look down at the forest that spread out in front of the buildings.

After the first culture shock of the cheek-kissing greeting, my next big surprise was with Czech food. It took me some time to get used to eating meals without rice, and so much bread, cheese and potato. The cold weather was also a massive shock, with local people commenting on how pleasant it was while I shivered in the thickest clothing I could find. It was such a contrast from low-land Cambodia where the weather rarely drops below 20 degrees. I could not understand how it was possible for anyone to survive the impending winter, with the -20 degree temperatures and ice and snow everywhere.

After a few days, I went to visit the university campus to register and to see where I would be spending my time. The flowerbeds and gardens that filled the open spaces were made even more beautiful by the adjacent state park. Walking through the well maintained and litter-free environment felt like a different world to chaotic of Phnom Penh.

While the natural beauty of my new home was easy for me to appreciate and adapt to, other aspects of Czech life were more difficult. As my first trip to a supermarket proved, learning to understand the new language (and how to pronounce it) was going to take time. Weather, food and greeting custom differences had all been shocks I had overcome and become familiar with, so I was confident I would succeed with all the other new challenges that I would face is this country so far from my family.

My lovely host family however, certainly helped make the Czech republic feel more like home. After one week in Hradec Kralove they invited me and another

Cambodian student, Monkol, to visit them in the capital city, Prague.

Luba, my host mother, was best friends with Eva, who had also collected me at the airport, and Eva was Monkol's host mother, so it was great to have such a friendly little 'family' for us to feel more comfortable.

They met us at the bus station, and took us to see the ancient Prague Castle, dating from the 9th century and perched high above the Vltava River, and the town that has been central to European history for over a thousand years. It was so different from anything I had seen before in my life; it felt as though I was in a dream or walking through a television show. In a sea of tourists from all over the world, it finally struck me that my dream to travel the world and experience all that was different from Cambodia had begun. It was actually happening.

The Prague visit happened to fall on my 18th birthday, and Luba had prepared a birthday cake for me. Not only was it the first time I had had one – such cakes are a very recent addition to urban Cambodian lives – but in order to visit their house, we had to take a short trip on a train, which also was a first for me.

The next day Luba and Eva took us exploring more of the old city, and then we all cooked Czech food together. Luba's fridge held more food than I had imagined possible, and the meal we made was so tasty that it helped calm my fears over having to eat Czech food for the next three years.

That afternoon they drove us back to our dorms, and while we passed lots of beautiful villages and fields, I spent much of the time napping like a little girl. The love shown by our host mothers was so genuine and warm. It was lovely to know we had a friendly family so close by.

In the first few months, this support was much needed. My Mongolian room mate had traveled with her husband, who also lived in our room. The stress of not knowing the local language got to me, and I missed my family at home.

While I had lots of studying to do, I was still able to experience social activities. In a long list of firsts during my time in the Czech Republic, I visited my first dance club, the 21 Club. In Cambodia such establishments were only in Phnom Penh, and frequented by the children of political and business elites. Yet many of my fellow students in Hradec Kralove went often and spoke excitedly of drunkenly dancing into the early morning.

In Cambodia, alcohol is largely drunk by men, not women, and so I was happy to only drink orange juice, and while I still managed to have a very interesting evening experiencing such a different culture, I did not feel the need to go back again very soon.

I had arrived in Autumn, and while my classmates noticed the falling golden leaves as the sign that winter was arriving, for me it was much easier. It gets so very cold! And with winter meant the impending arrival of snow, something I had only seen on television and was incredibly excited to see for myself. When it first fell, I ran around outside like a child, and lay down on what had been the grass in front of the dorm to make snow angels as I had seen in films. I still struggle to properly describe how exciting the experience was for me.

Christmas soon arrived, and once again, this was the first time I had celebrated the Christian holiday. I spent the time with my host family, and helped them decorate the traditional christmas tree, wrap presents and make festive foods for the big feast that is so central to the Czech celebration.

My first months in the Czech Republic had been fantastic, and I was very thankful that I had been given – and taken – this opportunity. The dreams and goals that had motivated me to study hard during school were slowly being realised. While some people are scared to achieve their dreams, as they do not know what to do afterwards, my experience only motivated me to dream higher, to think bigger, and to see and do even more.

Chapter 14: Women Should Not Travel Far

"Travelling is the best education that you will never learn in the classroom"

The cultural rules that have governed behavior of both men and women in Cambodia have existed for centuries. For women these are greatly more restrictive than for men, and nothing about their prescribed roles for women could be considered fun or liberating. I do not think that anyone who has not grown up experiencing these restrictions can understand life for Cambodian women.

Ever since I was young I had been told that it was not safe for women to travel far from home alone as it was not safe. This is one of the many 'rules' that has been passed from generation to generation. And while it is indeed true that there are dangers in the world, by staying at home and not daring to go out and challenge the society in which these dangers are allowed to exist, there will never be any change for the better.

Such fear has meant that women have been restricted and denied developing life experiences, while men have been allowed to explore the wider world and enrich their lives because of it. Are we totally helpless? Of course not, but the freedom to go out and confront such beliefs has long been denied most women.

My mother was given a brief glimpse through her early schooling, and that was enough to ensure that she pushed and encouraged me to do more than just accept my traditional position as a woman in Cambodia. She let me leave home by myself, and to face all of the challenges and possible criticism this would invite.

After going to university, first in Cambodia and especially once in the Czech Republic, I had the freedom to set my own rules to live by. The ability to travel where I wanted was now only limited by my funds, not the fears of older generations. I did not suddenly become a different person, but was able to ensure I was happier and more fulfilled.

Years of being treated as some kind of weaker person in the village, who had to constantly be looked after and watched simply for being a woman in a dangerous 'man's world,' had at times made me feel resentful of being born a girl. My brothers were not told it was unsafe to be out after dark, or to be careful in case they were raped.

Yet as I got older, my resentment shifted not to my sex, but to the idea that women were weaker and in constant danger. Why must we be taught to be fearful of the outside world? Why were my male classmates not being taught not to rape women instead?

After moving to Phnom Penh for university, I was of course anxious of the new challenges and dangers I faced away from my village, just as anyone moving to a new place is. But I did not let this fear cripple me, or stop me from exploring my new surroundings. I knew that I wanted to be there, that I needed to be there in order to further my aspirations to travel, and with that in mind everything became easier. Trial and error allowed me to grow as a young woman in ways impossible had I remained in the cloistered role of a village girl, and they better allowed me to make informed life decisions.

I did not blindly and recklessly seek danger or ignore advice. I learnt how to read maps, to plan financially and logistically, to find the best – and cheapest – transportation tickets, to be aware of cultural differences, and to be as prepared as possible for the unexpected events.

My travels have been an essential part of making me who I am today, however far that might be from the traditional 'proper Cambodian woman'. My travels have been the making of me. I know I can die happy with my memories from my trips, and all the risks I took.

I have never had much material wealth, and my adult life has only confirmed the importance of freedom and spontaneity, compared to the value that some people place on their televisions or cars.

I have learnt so much about different cultures, customs, food and people, and I feel this is translated into a greater respect for things that are different to my own.

When I was small, my grandfather predicted that my larger-than-normal feet were a sign that I would become a farmer, working outside all day. I am happy to say his prediction was incorrect, and I instead used my big feet to walk my own independent path.

This has not come without certain self-imposed hardships, but for me they have all been worthwhile and this life can become addictive. Once I have been to one new country, rather than satiating my travel urges, it fuels my desire to see more!

At the age of 26 I have traveled to 15 different countries: the Czech Republic, Poland, Germany, Austria, Slovakia, the UK, France, Italy, Hungary, the USA, Thailand, Vietnam, Malaysia, Myanmar and Laos. Not bad for a poor rural girl who used to stare up at airplanes and dream of where they flew to.

Despite all this travel, I have remained safe, and have seen and done things that my parents and classmates cannot even dream of. I have learnt to be strong, independent and inquisitive.

I have made a determined effort to avoid living my life like, to paraphrase an old Cambodian proverb, "like a frog down a well." I do not think that my world lies within the confines of a well, as I have seen for myself there is much more in this world.

I strongly believe that life is about choice, and the choice to make decisions for myself, whatever the consequences may be. As a woman in Cambodia, my life should not be constrained simply to living in the well as the frog, but everything should be available, and I am happy to say I am certainly not the frog.

Chapter 15: Respecting A Woman's Choice

"Women deserve to have a voice, and the choice to make their own decisions"

Stories normalising the role of women in Cambodian society have long been used for teaching young children about their expected roles in life. A famous 16th Century tale called Tum Teav is so popular that questions on it featured in my final high school exams, and it has been a part of Cambodian education since the 1950s.

The story starts with Tum, a handsome young monk, leaving his pagoda in Prey Veng province with his friend Pich, another monk who sells water containers made from bamboo. As they walk, villagers invite them to sing religious songs in exchange for food and accommodation, and Tum's beautiful singing voice coupled with Pich's expert flute playing, means that news of the musical duo spreads throughout the area.

While this was happening, a teenager named Teav was undergoing the 'Joul Malub,' or shade ceremony, during which young adult girls who have recently had their first period undergo up to three months of strict lessons on how to become 'good' women. This is where 'Chhab Srey,' the women's code, was taught, including such important life lessons as how to speak softly, not to look men directly in the eyes and the dangers of travelling far from home.

Teav's mother invited Tum to sing for her and her daughter, during which Teav fell in love with Tum, and he for her, but he had to return to his pagoda. However, Tum was so in love that he quit the priesthood, and went back to try to marry Teav.

After professing their love and sleeping together, Tum had to leave to sing for the King. During this time the son of the provincial governor decided he wanted to marry Teav himself, and her mother accepted, despite her protests. To make matters worse, the King had ordered his officials to find him a new concubine, and they of course found Teav, which ended her engagement to the governor's son, but did nothing to help Tum and Teav.

Tum only learned of these events after he was called to sing before the king's new concubine. His initial shock turned to anger, and he sang a song about the pair's love that caused Teav to cry. The king demanded an explanation for the song and the two told how they were in love, so eloquently in fact that the king permitted them to get married.

Now it was the turn of Teav's mother to be angry, and she returned to the village and plotted how she could have her daughter marry the governor's son as before. In the end she wrote a letter claiming to be very sick, and requesting Teav come visit her.

This she did, and was kept hostage by the governor's family in preparation for marriage, despite her already being married. When Tum discovered the trap, he told the king, who gave him a letter ordering Teav's release, but before he could present the letter, he was killed by the governor's soldiers. Upon hearing the news, Teav killed herself, and when the king learnt what had happened he was furious, enslaving the governor's family, and brutally killing the son and Teav's mother.

The story highlights the male-dominated society of Cambodia at the time, and the evil of greed and power. Teav's mother made decisions for her daughter that were in her own personal interests – marrying her off for wealth, not love – rather than what Teav wanted. Had her mother given her daughter the freedom to make her own life decisions, there would almost certainly have been less money and power in her life, but there would have been joy, and all would have lived to experience it.

I have always looked at this story and been thankful that my parents have been so different to Teav's mother. They have not attempted to marry me against my will, and have encouraged my freedom. While the story is historical, many of the scenes could easily have taken place in modern Cambodia. Arranged marriages still take place, where financial considerations continue to trump love and happiness.

Through reading books from around the world I have been exposed to different realities for women that do not necessarily conform to the strict and restrictive ones that Cambodian women face. While the girls in my village may have accepted the commands of their parents, I think this has much to do with a lack of knowledge of any alternatives. I am grateful to my parents, and my studies, for teaching me that there are always options.

I will not marry because of my age, or expectations to have children. I will not marry until I have found someone who I truly love and want to share the rest of my life with.

In Cambodian society, the fact that I did not marry before I turned 25 marks me as strange. I say that the opposite is in fact true. I think it is odd to be married so young, before one has had a chance to finish education, explore their surroundings and learn about what they find valuable in life. I would love to see all Cambodian women making such important life decisions about their futures by themselves, at a time they are comfortable with, not just following existing cultural norms.

Chapter 16: Our Male-dominated Society

"A community will live in peace when everyone has equal rights"

I know that there are many countries where the lives of women are worse than in Cambodia, but that still does not make it easy for us here in this male-dominated society. Growing up in an environment that is so strongly geared towards men has long motivated me to try and do something to rebel.

Women are also human, and make up more than half of the population of country, and yet news reports of men beating, raping and killing women is a daily occurrence. Such use of violence is clearly an attempt to cause fear, and exert some sort of dominance that should have no place in any society. All people have the same rights to live their lives as they choose, within the laws of their country, and without interference.

In my village growing up, it was an open secret which women were suffering domestic abuse from their husbands. One of our closest neighbors suffered horribly from her drunk husband, as did their children. When he was drunk, which was often, he would scream and curse her for any perceived inferiority, and there was nothing she could do to appease him.

It would often result in him beating his family, with the children running to hide out of fear. All of this could be heard in our house, yet no one did anything to stop it.

It did however instill in me a strong dislike of violence. He would destroy the items in the house, and I started to think that this was the power of alcohol, some sort of drink that made men violent and uninhibited.

Yet many women in similar situations do not seek police assistance or a divorce, but rather stay as the woman's code commands. Such reluctance to seek official support is also largely to due with financial concerns. In a society in which men control finances and land titles, they have great power over their wives. It is a scary prospect for a women to consider leaving the relative security of their home, even if it is abusive, if they do not have the education and life experience to start a new life somewhere else.

At school in Cambodia girls are taught how to behave like 'proper Cambodian women,' following mantra and beliefs passed down from older generations. But as I have written elsewhere, herein lies clear hypocrisy. The reality of Cambodian culture is that it is perfectly acceptable for men to have sex before marriage, and even with other women while married.

Men are traditionally compared to gold; and as such when they get 'dirty' they can simply be washed clean. Women on the other hand are likened to sheets of white linen that once soiled can never be washed clean again.

It is one example of many in Cambodia of men being able to do whatever they want, while women are stigmatised for similar behaviour.

I find these comparisons to be very distasteful. Telling women who have exercised independence in their lives that they are dirty and damaged and unable to get clean again is destructive. It forces women to be introverted and suppress their feelings and actions, rather than be adventurous and inquisitive. If any comparison to an object must be made, I would rather Cambodian women think of themselves as diamonds – valuable and precious, even if covered in mud.

I think it is important for women to remember this point. We live in a society in which sex workers are treated as some of the lowest, dirtiest people, and yet no questions are asked of the men whose money fuels this industry. Women hold the place of objects, not people capable of thought and action, such as the men believe themselves to be.

The same is true of the many thousands of young women employed in the countless KTVs found in every town in Cambodia. Each night women line up at the entrance to be 'chosen' by male patrons to sit with, dance and entertain them for the night.

They are chosen simply for their beauty, poorly paid, and discarded at the end of the night.

Maybe this is one reality of life for women in Cambodia.

Chapter 17: A 1,000 km Bicycle Journey

"Regardless of gender, you can do anything you want to do when you believe"

I challenged myself to ride across Cambodia

Sport is not as popular in Cambodia as in many other countries. Sure, the national stadium is always packed when the football team plays important international matches, but is almost empty for league games. People play volleyball, and older individuals may play boules – a holdover from the French colonial period – but in general it does not occupy the same level of attention as I have experienced in other countries.

This extends to more energetic forms of transport as well. Cambodians hate to walk anywhere, and with the availability of motorbikes at similar prices to good bicycles, most people do not cycle anymore either. Only the poorest, most rural villagers still cycle as their main means of getting around.

Easy credit from microfinance lenders means that few people lack access to funds to upgrade to a motorbike, or even a car. So anyone who cycles for choice is either pitied for being very poor, or thought of as crazy.

When my older brother was 19, he cycled his mountain bike from Phnom Penh to the coastal city of Sihanoukville, a journey of 240 km, in a day. Instead of receiving praise and encouragement, many people said he had shamed his family and even our uncle agreed. In all seriousness, people in the village questioned whether he was suffering from an mental disorder, as why would anyone cycle such a distance when the bus cost less than $8.

Another time, he took 10 days to run between Phnom Penh and Siem Reap in the north of Cambodia, a distance of over 300 km. He did it to raise money for his startup business, and while he received praise from many quarters, and was interviewed on television, our neighbours maintained he was crazy. And this is in a country where men are given more freedom to travel and to do strenuous activities than women.

So when it came time for me to do my own physical challenge, I knew that few people outside of my family would think I was sane. In 2013, I agreed to cycle 1000 km as part of a fundraising event for Cambodian education for PEPY organization. For 18 days, I cycled from Siem Reap City to the southeastern town of Kep. Without any training I had agreed to be one of the trip leaders, which meant that I was not just cycling, but had to look out for everyone else and ensure safety was maintained. I was also the first woman to have taken part.

It was by far the most physically challenging thing I had ever done, and the idea of cycling up to 100 km a day was daunting. But I was driven to help an organisation I supported, and wanted to prove to myself, and others, that a women was just as capable of doing this as anyone else. I would also get to explore parts of the country I had not yet seen.

Growing up in a rural village, free to explore the landscape and learn – sometimes painfully – from my mistakes, I know there is much to be gained from being outside rather than stuck only in a classroom. Not only did I learn a lot about myself on the trip, but it opened my eyes to the reality of lives in different parts of Cambodia.

The journey across the country gave me a deeper perspective of my own nation and culture. I realized that I was welcome in my own country. Life in the countryside is very simple, but people share their lives with one another, rather than money, and I was able to witness laughter and smiles almost everywhere we travelled.

It was especially obvious with children, many of whom would run alongside our bikes shouting "hello" with giant grins on their faces. In all my foreign travels I have not yet discovered such a welcoming atmosphere as in rural Cambodia. And yet the trip was not without its reminders that women still have a long way to go before they are deemed as equal.

At one point, we had all stopped to buy coconuts as a reward for a long hot day in the saddle, when a local man came and started laughing at me, asking if I was too tired to continue cycling with the foreigners. I remember thinking at the time that it was odd that he didn't also ask the same question of my male Cambodian co-leader. While the man had suggested that Cambodians could not cycle as well as the non-Cambodians, what he was actually implying was related to my female ability to keep up with men in physical endeavours.

I know I am not the first female to cycle far in Cambodia, and the country has a number of fantastic female athletes competing regionally and at the Olympics in a range of sports, but I was likely the first Cambodian female doing something like this he had met face-to-face.

By breaking out of the prevailing social expectations for womanhood I had hoped that I might have received positive comments, rather than ridicule, but I suppose I should have remembered how my brother had fared after his athletic endeavors. Still, I felt like challenging him to justify his behaviour, and asked him why he thought himself able to judge me, while he likely sat around being lazy much of the day while his wife did all the hard work. He had no reply, and we continued on our journey.

I find it increasingly difficult not to let my passion for gender equality bubble to the surface, especially when confronted by ignorance. It is hard not to speak out, but I feel it is important to fight where I can for the betterment of women in Cambodia.

For starters, I wish more Cambodians, male and female, would cycle across their country and engage with their fellow citizens. Not only might this give me more opportunities to lead groups, but it would be an insightful learning experience for all involved. Rural Cambodians will gain exposure to examples of increased female rights from their more urban cousins, while at the same time be able to demonstrate the happiness that is possible without a focus on material wealth.

Completing the 18-day journey was a huge physical and mental achievement for me, and I felt great pride in what I had accomplished. I took part in something new to me as a challenge to myself, not for anything else, but as I learnt along the way, my action was also challenging entrenched social norms.

Chapter 18: A Free-range Human

"It is acceptable to be yourself, and it is okay to be different, you don't have to live inside the system all the time"

I think, I could be described as a 'free-range human.' I was raised largely outdoors and in an environment where I had to fight to live the life I wanted to without much help or support.

After three years in the Czech Republic, and some of the best experiences of my life, I returned to Cambodia in August 2012 without a plan or a job. I tried working for a few different companies but always came across the same problems, namely the disdain that bosses felt for their staff. I did not want to work somewhere I did not like just for money, but rather somewhere I could feel passionate about my job.

So in June 2013 I went to work in a summer camp in the US state of Vermont. This marked my third continent I had visited, and for three months I was immersed in beautiful natural surroundings alongside a wonderful group of young girls. I used all the money I had earnt at the camp to travel in Asia before returning home, where I faced the same questions as before: What do I want to do with my life?

My older brother, who had asked himself similar questions, came to the rescue, and offered me the chance to manage his travel company.

It was the perfect solution to my problems. I would now be in a job where I could travel and support my passions, without a dominating boss. And this is what I still do to this day, sharing my experiences with the guests. My job feels like a holiday, and I have no complaints at all.

My brothers and I, like many children in our village and across rural Cambodia, grew up needing to use our own imaginations for entertainment, playing outdoors and using what we could find for toys. At the time, marketing from toy companies did not really reach us, and we were thankfully spared their claims of shop-bought joy and contentment.

And besides, from a young age we were seeking our own ways to make money, be it fishing, hunting for snails, or selling fruit. We knew what animals or plants were edible, and I am thankful for the life skills I learnt at that young age.

We grew up in houses built by people in the village, surrounded by the farms and livestock we relied on to survive. Life was simple and most things needed to be made and fashioned by hand. But while many people were resigned to the fact they would likely live their whole lives on the island, I always dreamed of more.

Dreams are free of course, but they provided me with the energy and motivation to work harder at school and in seeing ways to make money where I could, and it is fair to say that this hard work has paid off.

Cut off from much of the consumerism and advertising now increasingly common throughout Cambodia, we were spared the depression, anxiety and vulnerability that I feel they breed. Teenagers at my high school lacked the exposure to beauty trends (and the money to do anything about it) that has unfortunately led to the sexualisation of children. Many other teenage girls feel that their value can be determined by their looks, not their attitude or actions.

I was far too busy studying and working to be concerned with the latest hairstyle or fashion. The craze for skin whitening that is overtaking much of the 'non-white' world was thankfully unknown to us in the village. Given the number of hours we all spent outside, it would have seemed laughable to try to appear lighter skinned without the constant images of promoted pale Thai or Chinese celebrities.

Despite my Vietnamese and Chinese heritage (both traditionally lighter skinned than Khmer) I inherited my father's Khmer features – dark skin and big eyes. Since leaving the village many people, including friends, have suggested I lighten my skin to become more beautiful. I have grown sick of hearing such comments, even if they were well intentioned.

I cannot easily change other people's perspectives on the world, except by living my life how I wish. I can be happy and content and might just lead to a few others re-thinking their own actions and priorities. Women should not feel trapped by the constant need to look 'beautiful' – as defined by advertisers and television. We all have far greater worth than that.

True beauty is when one is able to look in the mirror and see confidence and strength reflected back. And it is this self belief that will help bring about gender equality in Cambodia, not an obsession with how we look and how we think men see us.

For me, happiness comes from staying true to myself, not forgetting experiences from my past and remembering what has driven me to live the life I do and become more of who I am.

I am the little girl who dreamed of leaving her small village and travelling the world, who managed to pass high school in a culture that did not push academic success for girls, who found ways to make money in whatever free time I could find. All of these things have made me 'me'.

Chapter 19: Seeing Is Believing

*"There are always choices in life,
you do not have to be stuck on a
dead end road"*

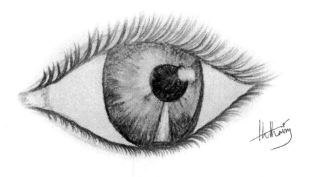

Visualize your dream and believing it

Most people find something far easier to believe if they can see tangible evidence of it, rather than relying simply on faith. In my efforts to show that it is possible to break from restrictions and social constrictions and live a fulfilling and independent life, just telling people it is possible has not been enough.

As I have stressed throughout this book, I have been very lucky to have two supportive parents, who have ensured that their children were given the chances in life that they had been denied themselves. And yet, after a certain point, I have had to maintain my own support for myself.

The biggest mental danger to success is not the hatred or envy of others, but self doubt within ourselves. Once negativity has crept into our thoughts, then it is far more likely that we will fail.

In life it can be almost impossible to control the thoughts of those around us – unless we cut ourselves off from everyone, which of course is not healthy – and so focusing on how we interact with the world and the good that our actions do is much more important. By being happy, and projecting this happiness, there is better potential for influencing others than trying to directly address them.

If I had followed the route set out for a 'proper woman' from my village, there is not a chance that I would be where I am today. I can almost guarantee that my life would now consist of farming rice, and living very close to where I grew up, in a small wooden house with a husband and a few children.

I would not have a university degree, not have flown in a plane or visited other countries let alone continents, not have been aware of some of the strong and powerful women who are in an unfortunately small number of positions of authority in Cambodia. As a society we idolise historic male kings and generals, yet the role of women in shaping the country is ignored, and this in turn provides few role models to aspire to. The limitations of the past still haunt the present.

If women are not challenging a society that fetishizes their beauty but does not celebrate their brains, then nothing will change. If we want to live in a country that respects us, where we are safe and can live as we choose, then we must push for change. Our politicians are almost all male and so are our business leaders, police and army officers and university professors. Why do they wish to change a society in which they are respected and well paid? Because we need to make them see that gender equality is in their best interests, as well as our own. In addition to the the basic human rights of women, we are half of the population and should therefore have half of the power to decide how our country is run and how the citizens live.

If there are no role models in this generation, who will we be able to inspire the next?

Girls and women need to be encouraged to push for more roles of authority in Cambodia, which will in turn encourage more to do the same. It always pains me to return to my village and see how many of the younger children, who I used to help with their English, are now married with children and follow their parents as farmers, without having at least experienced what else there is in this world available to them.

They are continuing the cycle of rural Cambodian life, ignorant that more is possible and that this cycle can be broken if they choose to do so.

Without the support of parents, and good teachers, it can be difficult to convince poor farmers that education is important, and worth paying for, especially in a society where corruption and family connections can still be more important than actual ability.

Current attitudes ensures that the cycle remains the same. Undereducated parents do not then tend to ensure their own children are better educated.

I want to change that.

I have pursued my education, both formally and through exploration, I have never paid a bribe to get a job – money to get a job. Indeed I have walked away from opportunities where I was asked to pay.

There are always choices and options in life, even if some seem much easier or more rewarding, and I never let myself think that I must do something just because there is no other way.

Few in my village imagined I would actually never succeed with my dreams, and if I or my parents had listened to their advice I never would have. They chose to support me in my education, even though sending me to work in a factory would have made their lives easier. They found another way to afford my education, and I can never thank them enough.

My mother, from her own regrets and frustrations, understood the value of education and ensured that we went to school. When our neighbors urged her to stop our schooling so that we could earn money for the family, she understood that the long term benefits would be greater if we stayed in school.

Since 2013, when I joined my older brother's travel company as operation officer, I have loved every minute of it. I have found the freedom to further pursue my travel dreams, while actually being employed! He obviously shared a similar childhood to me, and we have many of the same views on gender equality, the environment and how Cambodia can develop, and this is demonstrated in how Toursanak (our travel company) operates.

It has allowed us to start homestays in our village and experience the positives of rural Cambodia, and hopefully share their experiences and knowledge to help those in the village gain different perspectives of the world. The extra income for the families is also great, and we try to ensure this goes towards paying for the educational costs of any of the children at the host families.

Having foreign visitors, many of them students, come to the village and interact with villagers in their daily lives is something I truly believe benefits the village on so many levels, and I hope demonstrates the value of education to any who are still undecided.

I want to show that there are ways to make money in rural communities that do not have to involve working in factories or migrating to Thailand, that there is value in the traditional charm and hospitality of rural life that can have a positive impact on the community.

Being back in my own community has, I hope, proven that education is a great tool with which to fight against poverty, and that empowerment just takes innovation and new ideas. As long as people are united and willing to work together then almost anything is possible.

After eight years of leaving the village, more girls in the village have started to study English and more are staying in education longer. The belief of my parents that investing in my education was worth the cost and additional hardship has hopefully set an example for others in our village – and maybe one day beyond.

It is true that education is a long term investment, but I know that once someone has received it, one's life and country will never be the same.

Chapter 20: Become the Captain of Your Life

"You are the captain of your own life, you can sail in any direction you want to"

I have been lucky enough to speak about my experiences at events at high schools, universities, with NGOS and at a number of other events. I am always happy to note a large number of young girls in the audience, and I feel that sharing the journey I have taken to get to this point is especially meaningful. My message, as you have read in the book, is simple: hold on to your dreams and believe in yourself.

To any recent high school graduate in the audience, who might be unsure what to do next in their life, and lacking the necessary parental or community support, I am proud to be able to hopefully offer advice I hope resonates with them. It took me years to really define how I wanted my life to develop, and it was the guidance and advice of others that gave me the support and motivation to do so.

Finishing formal education anywhere in the world, is a difficult time for students. They have had their lives up to that point governed by the timetables of school, and the goal of graduating. From my own experience in rural Cambodia, the same is certainly true here as well. I found it difficult to find information about universities and classes, or any support in what I should study. Few people in my family, and certainly my community, had any experience with these questions. Despite the large number of new universities and colleges in Cambodia now, I still find there is a lack of access to clear and accurate advice on whether further education is the best avenue for someone, and if so, where and what to study.

This is especially true when it comes to female students. It is unlikely that their mothers attended university, or even graduated from high school, and there is therefore a level of parental support that is missing. Added to this is the wider lack of guidance for females in Cambodia to pursue their own desires and goals. Their lives are already predetermined by their sex; after school comes marriage, then babies and all of the work that raising children entails. Despite any personal aspirations a young woman might have, actually fulfilling them is certainly not easy.

This is not limited just to education and work. As my experience on the cycling trip showed, women are not expected to travel far from home or take part in sporting events. While there are notable exceptions to this – Cambodia's most successful athlete is a female taekwondo star – examples are few.

I once read that it is impossible to see the most beautiful view if one has not first climbed to the top of the mountain. I find this particularly inspiring. While there are achievements in life that may seem great, if they have not happened due to hard work and sacrifice then they are not truly the best that could have been achieved.

There are many people in life who have never "climbed the mountain," either because they do not want to, or because they feel unable to. But I strongly believe that one will gain the richest experiences, and rewards, only when striving to achieve the best, whatever obstacles may need to be overcome along the way. Having the courage to take risks in life, and the self confidence to believe in your own success, allows us to reach new heights in life, and the "views" are certainly worth it.

It is sad when girls do not believe that they are capable of achieving their dreams. While Cambodian women are in many ways lucky compared to other women in the world – there is no Female Genital Mutilation, we can drive and vote, etc. – life is certainly not equal, and we all must fight to live the lives we want, and not feel trapped by social pressures and ingrained habits.

Indeed, I have always tried to use the long-standing views that many Cambodians have of women to challenge them and force people to reevaluate what they have been told and believe. I present to the world the image of a strong and independent woman that I want others to see, and I hope that this inspires others to do the same.

I believe that having a role model is very important in helping to inspire us to pursue the things we want. They provide an example of someone who has managed to achieve their goal, thus proving that we can also do it ourselves. I find it strange to hear of celebrities called role models, because for me I do not find the fact that they are famous necessarily making them someone whose life I want to emulate. For me a role model must be a leader, someone inspirational, whose message is more important than their image, and as such Daniela Papi perfectly fits that criteria.

I met Daniela Papi when I was 17, which I described earlier in the book. She wasn't a celebrity, she wasn't famous, she was just working hard to make a difference in people's lives. She inspired me then to pursue the things I am most passionate about, and she continues to do this now, even after she has left Cambodia.

She believed in me, and provided examples on a daily basis of what a focused, independent woman can achieve.

Ever since I was a child I have always wanted to write books, to be read by people around the world. I think this was sparked when I was probably aged nine, and saw the photograph and short biography of the author of a book I had just finished. I cannot now remember the book or the author, but I knew from that point onwards that I wanted one day to see my own picture grace the back of a book as well.

In 2009, an educational NGO called Room to Read (RtR), which has a focus on producing affordable Khmer language books aimed at boosting reading and literacy amongst young rural Cambodians, chose a short story I had written to publish after I attended a writing workshop they hosted.

Three stories from each young author workshop they organise are chosen to be published. My story "The Little Parrot's New Shoes" was selected from thirty submissions, and I was elated that my dream to be a writer had come true. Not only that, but I would be helping rural Cambodians, such as I had once been, to hopefully gain a love of reading.

RtR invited me to attend a second workshop in September 2010, and once again my submission, this time titled "Flying Ruler," was chosen for the next year's book. I have continued to write ever since, although this book marks the first time I have written something autobiographical, and something so long!

I have been lucky enough, and well supported by friends and family, to be able to see my childhood dream become a reality, and I really hope that my story in turn motivates other young girls when it comes to making difficult decisions about their lives.

I have shared my story with audiences across the country, and hope that my message has inspired other girls to be stronger in pushing their convictions and achieving their dreams.

We are the captains of our own ships, life, and it is therefore up to us to steer them as close as we can to the direction we desire, whatever that may be. Yes there will be waves, and storms, but it is possible to reach the destination we have set ourselves, but only if we have self belief that we are capable of this, regardless of gender or background.

I believe we all have the necessary courage and strength, we just need to find it inside of ourselves. We have the ability to love, to share, and to help one another, and that these should be central to how we live our lives.

Life is a beautiful and wonderful gift, and we should make full use of the time on Earth we have.

Turn The Page To See Photos

The three generation of women. (Photo by Junette Burke)

My mother's arranged marriage

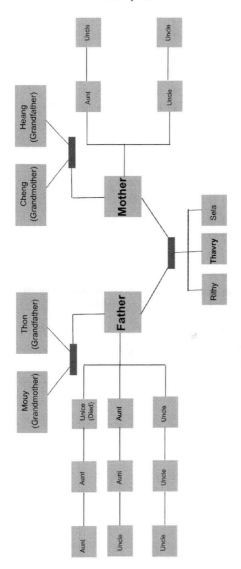

After my father recovered from malaria in 1993

When I was two and a half years old

I was teaching after school in the year of 2007

My Czech family celebrated my 18 birthday. My first time to celebrate a birthday

My life in the Czech Republic, I enjoyed the snow very much

My graduation day, June 26, 2012

I finally could make my dreams come true

My dream of travelling around the world has begun

I keep following my dream of travelling around the world

My journey of 1000 km by bike

I am now managing Toursanak, and starting to get involved with regional business-women

I speak about my experiences at events at high schools

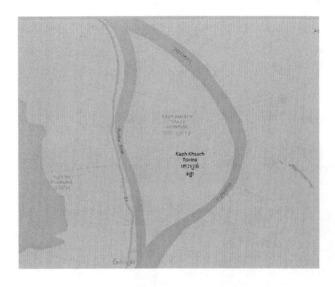

A map of Koh Ksach tunlea where I was born. By 2016, there are about 6400 people

My Gratitude To The Authors Who Inspired Me

It took me a long time until I had enough courage to write this book. Seven months in total to finish the first draft, and then three more months to get to the final version. I hope that my story will inspire others to feel empowered to be exactly who they are and to keep following their dreams.

Along the journey, I was inspired by many other authors and I will forever be grateful to them. I cannot fully express with words just how grateful I am. All I can say is that I have been moved deeply by their stories. To the following authors, thank you.

- *'Anne Frank: The Diary of a Young Girl' by Anne Frank.*
I was so transfixed reading Anne's secret diary. It motivated me to keep my own personal journal since 2007.

- *'First they killed my father' and 'Lucky Child' by Loung Ung.*
These books encouraged me to write about my mother and father's suffering during the Khmer Rouge. When she described her childhood before the Khmer Rouge and how she was so loved by her father I was shaken. I felt exactly the same way when my mother told me her story about her childhood.

- *'The Alchemist' by Paulo Coelho.*
This book taught me never to give up on my dreams, no matter how hard the journey.

- *'The Longest Ride', 'The Last Song', 'The Notebook', 'Message in a Bottle', and 'The choice' by Nicholas Sparks.*
All of these stories inspired me to dream bigger, to touch readers' hearts not just in Cambodia but all around the world.

- *'I am Malala: The Girl Who Stood Up for Education and Was Shot by the Taliban' by Malala Yousafzai.*
Malala's personal story drives me to fight for equality within my own country. I felt like our stories were so similar, how her father supported her education and how she inspired other girls to pursuing an education.

To the above authors I thank you for inspiring me to write A Proper Woman. I hope my book will inspire other readers around the world to tell their stories.

Thavry THON

Thavry Thon has received her bachelor degree from the University of Hradec Kralove, Czech Republic with a major in Information Management. She was born and raised in a very simple farming family on a remote small island on the Bassac River in Cambodia. Her family always supported her and valued education very much. They encouraged her to pursue higher education in the hope of having a better future. Her parents always told her that 'education' is the key to success and will reduce poverty in Cambodia.

Thavry is currently the Managing Director of Toursanak Adventures, where she is active as a travel blogger, a translator, and a trip leader. She is also an international educator, and the author of four books. She published two children's' books in 2010 and 2011 with Room To Read, and an inspirational book with a Taiwanese company in 2013. She continues to enjoy travelling within Cambodia and abroad.

Peter FORD, Editor

Peter Ford came to Cambodia in 2014 to work at the Khmer Rouge tribunal. He stayed, and has spent much of the past two years as a journalist and editor.

He grew up in England and has a Masters degree in Geopolitics and Security from King's College, London. He has lived in Japan, Kazakhstan, Sierra Leone and Senegal, has travelled to almost 50 countries, and is well aware he has many more to go . He has seen more of Asia than Thavry, although she is quickly catching up. He can often be found on a bicycle looking hot and tired.

I also wish to thank the other contributors to the book

PISITH YEEN, book cover art and book layout. Your talent for design has been invaluable, and I am very thankful for the fantastic book cover you have created.

Designer
Email: pisith.yeen@gmail.com
FB: www.facebook.com/PisithYeen

SIPHENG LIM, book cover photo shoot, thank you for the beautiful portrait photo shoot. You have a great talents, and I am very happy to see how you are growing up everyday. I am very honored to be your non blood sister.

Photographer
Email: siphengl@gmail.com
FB: www.facebook.com/siphengl

SREYMAO SAO, sketches. Your help advising me on the drawing has been a great help. The amazing art has added more flavour to this book, and brought them to life. Thank you for being such a great friend and travel partner.

Artist
Email: saosreymao@gmail.com
FB: www.facebook.com/sreymao.sao

ERIC JENKINS-SAHLIN gave me very critical feedback and asking so many questions to improve my book.

JESSICA ARMSTRONG who helped me with my last minute of the gratitude page.

IAIN DONNELLY helped me with my last revise edition and answering so many of my doubt about writing journey.

Thank you also to **MARK BOLAM** for helping to proofread the book and helping with the last bit of editing. Your kindness and contribution to this book has meant a lot for me.

Keep in Touch:

Follow my journey about A Proper Woman and my personal adventures. I always post updates about my travels, stories and inspiring stories I learn along the journey call "Life".

Contact the author
Email: thavry@gmail.com
Website: www.thavry.com

Future Project: "A Proper Woman, in Khmer Language"

I believe that the story should be read by as many Cambodian people as possible, especially girls. I believe that they could absorb the story better through reading it in their own language.

In April, I will start to work on the Khmer version. It will take me a minimum of 6 months from writing to production. This English version took me 10 months to complete.

In order to make this project happen, I need your help. Every single dollar counts. If you would like to support me in my quest to inspire millions of other Cambodians, you can contribute to:

Paypal: thavry@gmail.com

Direct Bank Transfer:
SWIFT Code: ABAAKHPP
Beneficiary Account #: 000094153
Beneficiary Account Name: THON THAVRY
Beneficiary Street Address: No. 17 street 604, Toul Kork
Beneficiary City/Country: Phnom Penh, Cambodia

Other ways you can help!

Tell your friends, family, and colleagues to help by buying the English version of my book, so that I can generate some income and have more time to focus on writing the Khmer version.

Your support is the bridge to inspire those countless girls and other Cambodian people who still doubt about their dreams and future.

Made in the USA
Columbia, SC
22 September 2023